REPRESENTING THE MARGIN

REPRESENTING THE MARGIN
Caste and Gender in Indian Fiction

Dr. Ajay S. Sekher

PUBLICATIONS
KALPAZ PUBLICATIONS
DELHI-110052

Representing the Margin : Caste and Gender in Indian Fiction

Rs. 690

ISBN: 81-7835-690-2

Published in 2008 in India by
Kalpaz Publications
C-30, Satyawati Nagar,
Delhi-110052
E-mail: kalpaz@hotmail.com
Phone : 9212729499

Laser Type Setting by: Quick Media, Delhi
Printed at : Singhal Print Media, Delhi

Dedication

To Prof. P P Raveendran my teacher, Arun my brother and friends who supported me in this endeavour.

Contents

This book is about the representation of socio cultural margins of caste and gender in works of fiction written in various Indian languages in the twentieth century, basically in the postcolonial contexts. It takes representative samples from Hindi/Urdu, Bengali, Kannada, Malayalam and English.

It would be appropriate to elaborate the context in which this study was formulated and explored. Soon after my M AI got a chance to work in the Government service in the Panchayat department in Kerala. We Keralites boast of. our modernity, renaissance and social progress. But at the bottom things are still barbaric and dismal. The very system established for decentralization and democracy at the grass-root level was found to be the most feudal and orthodox anti people establishment.

If Dalit Bahujans who are appointed by the Government Commission cannot work'in the public service with dignity and self respect how can the system serve the marginalized people in need? The case is not different in any other department or in public sector at large. In parts of Kerala, as elsewhere in the country where traditional cultural monopoly groups are influential even constitutional systems are doctored and policed by them. Brahmanical Savarna-Syrian lobby is exercising critical policy making power and leverage in public service despites the safeguards.

The hegemonic and status quo interests of the power elite are once again exposed in the current Social Studies text book controversy. Discrimination, double-dealing and psychological intimidation and suppression of the marginalized is an everyday reality in our public offices and state departments. My teaching experience in primary schools to universities also endorses the evil proportions of anti reservation and anti Dalit Bahujan discourses propagated by the monopoly groups who just can't share power and resources. Caste based verbal assault and dehumanizing discourses are incommunicable. All these symbolic atrocities are choreographed in a covert but strategic manner. It is part of the symbolic and epistemological violence that the hegemonic ideology of Brahmanism has been, inflicting on the people, the subaltern.

Affirmative action is the real issue of desire for the traditionally advantageous groups. Their neo Brahmanic economic determinism is built on an erasure of the history of injustice and inequality. In this covetous campaign for economic reservation they are even getting the support of the left oriented who are caste-blind and class-obsessed. Historical, social and educational backwardness created through centuries of Savarna discrimination against the Dalit Bahujan people, that is the basis of constitutional reservation, is gradually obliterated and in place a neo Savarna-suffering myth is floated.

As a student of literary and cultural historiography I was challenged into intellectual enquiry and epistemological action in the milieu of resurging hegemony. When I looked around I found the hegemonic discourse engulfing the whole culture and society. It is ruling the minds, the movies, the media, the academia, the broadcasts, literature, textbooks, pedagogy, the legislature and the whole order of signs like language and representation. Resigning the job I pursued my doctoral research about the representation of socio-cultural marginality in Indian fiction. As I was working within the discipline of English I had to limit the scope and purview of the study in a genre. The gravest political issues of Indian cultural history and contemporary society confronted me in the form of caste and gender. It became part of a social struggle and cultural politics for democracy, representation and justice. It is a humble effort towards the democratization of culture and epistemology.

Even after fifty years of constitutional democracy the hegemonic potential of the dominant ideology still holds in our country and the Dalit Bahujan and women's question remains unresolved. The situation becomes worse when new kinds of cultural and spiritual nationalist avatars of Neo Brahmanism make their second^coming in the late twentieth and early twenty first centuries. The present attempt at analyzing specimens of fiction to see how they narrativize, textualize and problematize these vital socio cultural and political questions of our times and contexts therefore is not just an academic exercise, but is a cultural emergency and part of an inevitable cultural studies initiative.

The focus of enquiry and the thrust of the analysis of the present study would be on the narrativization of these questions in representative texts of fiction. What are the socio political and cultural implications and underpinnings of the representation of marginalization in the medium and genre of fiction, what could be the politics, ethics and aesthetics of such narration, how far such representations are subversive or consensual/complicit, what are the limitations and pitfalls of such intervening radicalism in fictional narration - all these questions are taken up in detail in the analyses. In the greater sense this enquiry is also a critique of modernity and its discontents as it analyses the dialectics of modernity, its radical as well as reactionary aspects. A problematic premise of contextualizing the text and textual izing the context would also be prominent in the attempt.

I hope this work will be useful in pursuing further studies and research in the field of contemporary literature, culture and society. The analysis of the politics of representation opens up a range of new problems and possibilities for the critically and socially inclined. I would like to term this an articulation of critical consciousness and an anticipation of the democracy of the future. After all it is a collective and cumulative work in ethics and epistemology, it is there because my fellow beings supported me in doing it. I would greatly acknowledge the support of Prof. P.P. Raveendran, Prof. V.C. Harris, Arun and other friends.

July 2008 **Dr. Ajay S Sekher**

Introduction: On the Margin

> Marginality, a suspicion that what is at the centre often hides a repression.
>
> Gayatri Spivak, "Explanation and Culture: Marginalia"

As a product of post-enlightenment democratization and capitalist development, fiction is linked to its discursive context, across languages and cultures.[1] With its dialogic potential and plurality of perspectives, it also uniquely signifies the multiplicities and complexities of the narrated realities. As a narrative mode of enquiry it is concerned with the peripheries and margins of the represented reality and the signified world of human experience, as it expands its boundaries further on and on into the less known and the less represented. A profoundly ethical and democratic concern and subversive radicalism could be identified at the core of fiction's representational politics.[2] The present study attempts an analysis of the representation of socio cultural margins of caste and gender in Indian contexts in works of fiction written in various Indian languages, taking representative samples from Hindi, Bengali, Kannada, Malayalam and English.

Using the classic metaphor of Don Quixote, Michel Foucault in *The Order of Things* problematizes the margins and boundaries of similitude, resemblance and representation in an attempt to make an epistemological critique of the act of representation. Foucault says that Quixote is both writing and representation. Quixote reads the world in order to prove the texts and the proofs that he gives are the glittering reflections of resemblances. His whole journey is a quest for similitudes and signs. "The signs of language no longer have any value apart from the slender fiction which they represent. The written word and things no longer resemble one another. And between them, Don Quixote wanders off on his own."[3]

Commenting on Cezanne's well-known statement on the act of representation - "I owe you the truth in painting and I will tell it to you," - Jacques Derrida says that the act of representation is a "highly precarious" one since truth could only be understood in terms of "presentation, representation, unveiling or adequation." This complexity would only result in unlimited possibilities of presentation and representation.[4] Thus the act of representation is a complex and problematic one that involves mediation by a subject in a given context of history, culture and locality. It involves intervention and doctoring in sign systems as well as in modes and media of communication. It requires potential coding, decoding and recoding across semiological frontiers and ideological and discursive paradigms.[5] It is not neutral and transparent, but is highly complex and contextual. It articulates the tensions and conflicts of the subjectivity in particular discursive contexts of history, under the influence of prevalent ideological formations and the compulsions of material reality.

Taking up the question of literary representation in his conversations with Edward Said, Raymond Williams observes that "representations are part of history, contribute to history, are active elements in the way that history continues; in the way that forces are distributed, in the way people perceive situations, both from inside their own pressing realities and outside them."[6] He adds that the method of analysis of representations could be tested historically and politically in diverse situations. For him analyzing the text is a way of finding new methods of discovering the relation between its constituents and its contexts, and is intimately wedded to the project of cultural studies. All these once again tell us about the socio cultural, political, economic and historic forces that determine this precarious act of mediation involved in representation; of shading and emphasis, of foregrounding and back grounding, of veiling and exposing, of the autonomy and tyranny of narration, and the need for its cultural, historic and contextual analysis. Narrative representation of the material reality and its hermeneutics are therefore fundamentally and finally political and positional.

Redefining the pedagogy of the humanities as the arena of explanation that questions the (legitimate) explanations of culture, where culture is a process rather than an object of study, Gayatri Spivak observes that marginality is a suspicion that what is at the centre often hides a repression.[7] According to her, deconstruction teaches us to question all kinds of transcendental idealism and repressive violence, especially in hegemonic discourses and ideological narration. The models of legitimate and dominant culture are often hegemonic and repressive, engaged in othering and excluding sites of contesting and subversive cultures. Thus the act of narration, whether it is historiographical or fictional, is highly problematic in the contexts of marginalization.[8] In India social exclusion, economic deprivation and cultural and political marginalization/ subordination were effected on the lines of caste and gender under the hegemonic ideology of Brahmanic Varnasramadharma.[9] The vast majority of people outside the fourfold Chathurvarnya system, the Bahujans, the Dalits and the women of all castes, were denied basic human rights and elemental human status for millennia under this most perverted and fascist ideological formation and its repressive regime. Even after fifty years of constitutional democracy the hegemonic potential of this ideology still holds and the Dalit Bahujan [10] and women's question remains unresolved. The situation becomes worse when new kinds of cultural and spiritual nationalist avatars of Neo Brahmanism make their second coming in the late twentieth and early twenty first centuries.[11] The present attempt at analyzing specimens of fiction to see how they narrativize, textualize and problematize these vital socio cultural and political questions of our times and contexts therefore is not just an academic exercise, but is a cultural emergency and part of an inevitable cultural studies initiative.

The Dalit Bahujan resistance movements in India could be contextualized in the historical, epistemological and material conflicts between the hegemonic Brahmanic ideology and praxis and the counter-hegemonic Dalit Bahujan cultures from outside the margins of the Hindu world.[12] In a larger democratic perspective it could be seen as a historically excluded and marginalized people's ethical struggle for social equity and democratic and civil rights.[13] The Brahmanic Varna system and caste hegemony are therefore key elements that should be critically analyzed in developing a subaltern consciousness that arises from a sense of historical suppression and past wrongs, which continue to be relevant even today.[14]

Brahmanism is analyzed contextually in the study as an ideology, a discourse and an institutional form of hierarchical inequality and cultural subordination. The discourse of the Brahman-centred religious obscurantism has its origin in the Vedic ages. In his essay "Early Brahmans and Brahmanism," D D Kosambi says that, early Brahmanism propogated a belief that "Brahman is a descendent of Brahma" himself and whenever Brahmanism is in peril "Vishnu is incarnated to protect it."[15] Buddhism was a critique and reaction against its decadent forms. As a parasitic ideology it creates a self-centred world/view and a consensual sense of cultural and ethnic supremacy. There is no egalitarian space and acknowledgement of the other in this discourse. It is another name for hierarchy in its social manifestations. It is one of the ancient forms of priestocracy and cultural elitism. Monopolizing and policing culture, writing and epistemology are its fundamental practices. There is also an element of pedantry and knowledge/power monopoly in the related discourses. Purity-pollution practices and engendered and embodied classification and hierarchization are its chief tenets. The divide-and-rule strategy has been its chief diplomatic agenda in maintaining the internal imperialism for thousands of years. The Varna theory is its instrument for social stratification which eventually gave birth to the caste system. The Brahman heads the fourfold Varna structure and below him are the Kshatriya, Vysia and Shudra . Kshatriyas must ensure the safety of the Brahman and the cow. The Shudras and the women must serve them as earthly gods. The Chandals and the followers of other religions are not even given human status in the Brahmanic imagiNation.[16]

The plural and broader movements of the real majority of people who were always outside the cultural geography of the Brahmanic nation could be placed and understood as the cultural and democratic revolution that has changed and is still changing the society and polity in India. This began with the historic critique of hegemonic Brahmanism in Buddhism and continued into the subsequent Shramana critiques, including those of Kapila, Charvaka, Kabir, Phule, Narayana Guru, Periyor and Ambedkar.[17] Any related epistemological attempt naturally aims at the development of a subaltern hermeneutics and praxis that emphasizes social justice and the voice of the suppressed, with elaborate and ground level deconstruction and reconstruction of epistemological and methodological systems and processes including historiography and pedagogy.[18] It should again be seen in the light of the radical and historic critiques of homogenizing and hegemonic nationalist discourses that patronized and represented the country from the days of the Gandhian nationalist movement onwards, suppressing the inevitable, irreducible signification of the diversity and plurality of people/cultures in this country.[19]

Though the critique of Brahmanism dates back to Buddhism, the consolidation of the collective political formation of the marginalized people in India is a fairly recent phenomenon.[20] It is a post-Mandal, post-Ayodhya and also post-Gujarat development. The Mandal commission report[21] which came up for consideration and national debate in 1990 radically exposed the immensity of the exclusion of Bahujans from the corridors of power/political representation and the monopoly of hegemonic groups in the high altars of constitutional state and democracy. This confirmed the warning of Ambedkar expressed more than half a century ago that transfer of power to the nationalist elite and the political mode of nationalism would only be a transfer of power to the regional Savarna hegemony.[22] The Anti-Mandal barbarism and riots unleashed by the status quo groups once again proved that internal colonization and sustenance of hegemony is an everyday reality.[23] The demolition of the Babri Masjid at Ayodhya in 1992 saw the pro-fascist mobilization of Bahujans by the same advocates of cultural and religious nationalism who eliminated the father of the nation soon after Independence. 2002 saw the culmination of this Hinduization drive in the Gujarat genocide in which thousands of Muslim minorities were literally burned alive. The coming of age of Indian Hindu fascism has therefore a historical itinerary of sustained hegemony and internal colonization over the Bahujan masses at the cultural and religious levels, with its ideological and discursive underpinnings in Brahmanism and its Varna, Caste systems of social stratification.

As was suggested earlier, the resistance to Brahmanism too has a long history which now converges on the polarization of the others and outcastes of hegemony against the cultural nationalism led by the Brahmanic elite, the nation state and its apparatuses monopolized by historically advantaged Savarna groups and their legitimized cultural nationalist discourses. The rise of the lower castes in North Indian politics and the emergence of Dalit Bahujan politics along with a nation wide alliance of minorities, women and low castes, both Scheduled Castes/ Scheduled Tribes and Other Backward Communities, could be situated in this larger emancipatory political formation, which could only be termed as a decentering, inclusive and rethinking critique of democracy from below. The old and inadequate (often Brahmanic/hegemonic in effect) conceptualizations of 'identity politics and Sanskritization' are contested and overruled here in the material and historical contexts of the peoples' struggle for social justice and equity as well as for democratic, civil and basic human rights. The homogenizing reductionism and stereotyping of the Hindu/Brahman-centered and referential gaze, that looks upon the collective movements and mobility of the historically marginalized for equal rights and historical shares in a democratic society as mere 'identity politics and ethnic mobility' is itself hegemonic, totalitarian and fascist since it silences/evades and oversteps profound questions of ethical, democratic and historical implications in the contexts of unlimited and unimaginable barbarism and shameless brutality for centuries. It is the old weapon that the 'secular and liberal' Savarna spokesmen of the ancient hegemony still use against the victims of history. This strategy uses the weapon of caste itself to defuse the subaltern classes' radical consolidation and dissociation from the hegemonic value sphere and meta-referential structure, by marking resurgence and dissociation as conformist caste craving for upward mobility within the hegemonic social structure. This is the significance of theorizations like "Sanskritization" that explain mobility within the Hindu caste/Varna order. They do not explain the dynamics of human communitizations.[24] Such theorizations can only be seen as attempts from the top to explain the hegemonic and totalitarian potential of colonized and appropriated epistemological processes that multiply inequality and sustain hegemony and even monopolize the whole discourse of human sciences practices in India,[25] providing striking resemblances to the knowledge/power discourses of Brahmanism.

Such an epistemological impasse created by the appropriation of the humanities and the academia for purposes of power and perpetuation of consensual hegemony, demands radical readings of social texts that are resisting and subversive, and which take position with the people and intervene radically in cultural politics and are liberative in the material sense. An analysis of the representation of marginality on the lines of caste and gender in fictional narratives across the country is taken up as a counter hegemonic task of resistance under these premises.

Socio-cultural categories of caste and gender in the Indian context of Brahmanic patriarchy are so inseparable in their material manifestation that they can not be analyzed in exclusion.[26] The vital questions of the gendered subaltern and subaltern patriarchy complicate the whole picture.[27] The older approaches isolating caste and gender inequalities have already come under scathing criticism.[28] The new political agenda being articulated by Dalit Bahujan feminists also demands the exploration of their shared and entangled histories and cultural contexts.[29] New inter-disciplinary enquiries by Dalit Bahujan theorists and Dalit Bahujan feminists raise complex questions on how we might understand the vital history of caste as a form of identification and as a structure of disenfranchisement and exploitation and on how we can revisit the forgotten and repressed histories that would contribute towards the development of a Dalit Bahujan feminist critique and subaltern hermeneutics that could radically address questions of inequality and repression.[30] The demand for historicizing the structures of forgetting and exposing the hidden histories of hurt and humiliation animates the contemporary claims for including caste as a significant category of social life, as an intimate and embodied form of sociality[31].

In the current conjuncture feminism in India responds to the gendered manifestations of caste inequality through its reorientation towards social transformation on an egalitarian basis. According to scholars like Anupama Rao this would involve a reexamination of gender and caste relations in such a way as to suggest that understanding the changing manifestations of caste is fundamental to the understanding of the particular forms in which gender inequality and sexed subordination are produced and grounded.[32] The objective is not a mere inclusion and rehabilitation of the marginalized, but involves a broader struggle for democracy, equality and social justice that would reinstate agency and mobility for the historically marginalized.

The current exploration also identifies caste as gendered and embodied under these complex discursive and analytical paradigms. The notion of patriarchy is also pluralistic with all sorts of socio economic and capitalist manifestations and role shifts in the present. Caste is also seen as sexed and connected to desire and defilement with its base in the purity-pollution practices of Brahmanism. It is also contextualized as a form of institutionalized inequality, a legitimate means of socio political control and regulation of kinship, a religio-ritual form of identity and subjectivity, a form of social engineering through taboos and the metaphysics of purity and touch. It even controls sexuality and love. The conceptual categories of the gendered subaltern, and the new subaltern as formulated by Gayatri Spivak, her own extension of the whole debate of Gramscian hegemony and the notion of Brahmanic patriarchy advanced by Uma Chakravarty, are also important in the following analyses.[33]

The focus of analysis in the present study would be on the narrativization of these questions in representative texts of fiction. What are the socio political and cultural implications and underpinnings of the representation of marginalization in the medium and genre of fiction? What could be the politics, ethics and aesthetics of such narration? How far such representations are subversive or consensual/complicit? What are the limitations and pitfalls of such intervening radicalism in fictional narration? All these questions are taken up in detail in the analyses. In a broader sense this enquiry is also a critique of modernity and its discontents, as it analyses the dialectics of modernity, its radical as well as reactionary aspects.[34] A problematic premise of contextualizing the text and textualizing the context would also be prominent in the attempt.

Fictional texts from five Indian languages including English (two texts from each language) are incorporated in the study to ensure regional and linguistic representation within the limits of the availability of works in translation. Since the Malayalam works chosen do not have published translations in English, I have translated the quoted extracts myself. In order to ensure adequate and just explication of the texts chosen and to avoid the mix-up of linguistic, literary and contextual elements of these five languages/literatures/cultures, works in each language are analyzed in separate chapters. A series of cross-textual and inter-textual significations, references and comparisons also provide linkages and coherent continuity to the connected episodes that sustain and develop the major arguments and themes.

A brief overview of the chapters would be appropriate here. The first chapter "Caste in Religion: *Godan, Song of the Loom*" analyzes the Hindi/Urdu works Godan by Premchand and Song of the Loom by Abdul Bismillah. The close textual/contextual reading focuses on the representation of caste inequality that exists across religions, whether majority or minority. The purpose of the enquiry is to identify the hidden ideology and hegemonic discourse that perpetuate this hierarchical inequality. Premchand was the first major and mainstream novelist to take up the question of the untouchables and Dalits in the North Indian Hindi/ Urdu context of rural and feudal Brahmanism in the early decades of the twentieth century. His representation of the Bahujans and peasant women, toiling and struggling for survival under caste lords and their repressive regime in the rural hamlets and darker sub realms of this vast country, was a socialist-realist attempt to voice the voiceless and to represent the unrepresented reality of the times. One might wonder why the product of such a pioneering attempt as *Godan* prefers to be content with a complicit resolution? The first chapter asks this question that connects the caste issue with culture and religion and explicates the dynamics of the Brahmanic caste hegemony in *Godan*. Examining the problem of caste and gender inequality among the minority Muslims of North India, especially among the Bahujan Muslims represented by the Ansaris of Benaras, in Abdul Bismillah's *Song of the Loom*, the chapter uncovers how the hierarchical ideology of Varnadharma has colonized all religions and cults in India. Even the new religion is of little help in countering this ancient hegemonic discourse that is in place in all walks of social and domestic life. The chapter also looks closely at the problematic and potential of narrating the plurality and inter linkages of the margins and subalternity, for the purpose especially of identifying the new and radical significations of liberation and resistance it opens up in contemporary political formations.

The second chapter "Brahmanic Patriarchy: *Rudali, Woodworm*" that deals with two Bengali texts (*Rudali* and *Woodworm*), traces the engendered and embodied premises of hegemony and an anticipated emergence of a new mode and praxis of articulation from the marginalized within the marginalized. The subaltern woman is the gendered embodiment and ultimate victim of Brahmanic patriarchal ideology and its various material manifestations, the margin within the margin. By representing and anticipating the complex and puzzling premises of the possibility of a subversive and counter-hegemonic speech from this newly awakened subaltern, Mahasweta Devi intervenes in the debate with her lifelong legacy of struggle and resistance to caste-patriarchy with a class perspective. The chapter also tries to explore critically the limits and liabilities of class analysis and theories based on mere economic determinism. The analysis of the sovereign subjectivity of Brahmanic patriarchy in *Woodworm* develops the caste/gender praxis of enquiry and further explicates the fascist, oedipal core of Brhamanism through a radical rereading of Sirshendu Mukhopadhyay's novel. The chapter exposes the disguised and metaphoric presence of patriarchal and casteist ideology in operation in a modernist text that only peripherally deals with questions of identity crisis and alienation. What was literally repressed and silenced in the text resurfaces with a vengeance to overshadow and engulf the whole narrative. The critique also foregrounds the repressive and exclusivist politics of masculinist and casteist practices dominating Indian narrative modernism.

The third chapter "Revisiting the Village: *Samskara, Gramayana*" attempts to read the canonical Kannada novels *Samskara* and *Gramayana* to expose the working of the caste-Swaraj Indian village, mythicized and celebrated in narrative representations. U R Anantha Murty's novel *Samskara* is analyzed by placing it in its historic and cultural contexts. Despite its depiction of the decadence of Brahmanism, the text of *Samskara* reiterates an ideological agenda of cultural elitism and textualizes the obscurantist metaphysics of the superior second birth, present at least in the subconscious stream of the narrative. The critique of the representational politics of modernism is continued here. It is also argued that the text narrativizes a male Brahman-centred worldview, which excludes women and Bahujans as "others." The reading of Rao Bahaddur's *Gramayana* that follows breaks apart the stereotypes of the polyphonic rural narrative after placing it in the context of the caste system and rural patriarchy. The totalizing discourses that categorize the whole feudal peasantry and village communities as subaltern in dominant and fashionable postcolonial deliberations, monopolized by the third world elite, too is contested here. The grass root level, micro-operations of Brahmanic hegemony that works in tandem with religion and gender politics become visible in this textual analysis. It also exposes the violence involved in such reductive characterizations as 'village epics and rural mythologies.' The chapter reveals the plight of the really marginalized and eternally subjected within this so called periphery, problematizing the whole debate of subaltern and village post-coloniality.

The fourth Chapter "Community and the Tribal: *Thalamurakal, Mavalimantam*" reads the two Malayalam novels *Thalamurakal* and *Mavelimantam* and looks in detail into the narrativization of the processes of communitization that leads to an erasure of sub caste divisions and Dalitization, a movement that cancels the hierarchical desire of caste and Varna. Both movements are discussed here as counter-hegemonic and emancipatory movements from below, especially in the contexts of peoples' resistance and the democratic politics of Mandalization. While narrativizing the plurality of struggles of a family in Palghat in eastern Kerala across generations against caste inequality, O V Vijayan's novel interrogates vital issues ranging from Brahmanism, nationalism, the Dalit Bahujan movements, Dalitization, conversion, communitization and 'Sanskritization.' The analysis places the fictional text in its discursive context to specifically look at the novel's handling of the caste question. The strategies of representing and articulating the subaltern subject and the politics and history of the subaltern resistance to meta-narratives and hegemonic discourses are dealt with in detail. The chapter also provides critiques of Sanskritization and Hinduization. The association between the caste question and the Adivasi question and the representation of tribals in K J Baby's *Mavelimantam* are also discussed in this chapter. Against the prevalent eco-tribal activist discourse the Adivasi crisis is situated right in the heart of the larger ideological and historical formations of Brahmanism. The analysis of this Malayalam narrative that claims to represent the tribal from closer quarters is also meant as an explication of the politics of the tribalism discourse and its primitivizing and genocidal intentions. The discussion lights up the problematic of fictional representation, narrative intervention and the erasure of historical contexts.

The fifth chapter "Nation Versus Conversion: *Kanthapura, The God of Small Things*" provides a critical account of imagiNation and the margins of imagination as they impinge upon the process of narration. It also attempts a critique of the representation of caste in conversion, because caste is often the un-representable in the process, especially when one converts to a "casteless" religion. In the larger sense conversion could be read as a critique of the Nation and its homogenizing narratives. Conversion is writing back from the margins of the modern nation and its meta-narratives of erasure and totalizing order. It is an act of defiance that threatens the cultural nationalist/pro-fascist foundations of the Nation. A pioneering narration of the nation, *Kanthapura*, by Raja Rao is reread here. The patronizing and paternalistic ideology of Gandhi's "Harijanodharana" and the related legitimizing discourses of nationalism are identified in the narrative text. The nationalist agenda is identified as the redeeming Brahmanic agenda that operates through the iconic character of the protagonist and his experiments with spiritual/religious/ cultural nationalism. The dilemmas and splits of the nationalist Brahmanic subject in representing the nation, overstepping the real majority of people, too are decoded from the textual surface here. As a politically significant act narration assumes the monopoly of the unconscious of the common people, the subaltern classes, and could become a cheap weapon of cultural neo-nationalism/s or even of fascism. For the Bahujans in India from the time of the Buddha, alternative religions have been liberation theologies that provide some kind of an asylum from the forces of cultural elitism and nationalism. The Dalit Bahujan converts constitute the vast majority of Indian minorities. Even the Constitution upholds conversion as part of one's religious freedom. But the key question is not of religion but of caste. What happens to caste in conversion, can one change caste as one's religion? What is your caste status after conversion to a new faith and a new community? All these are peripheral questions articulated, once again, touching upon the harsh reminder that there are only caste Hindus, caste Christians, caste Muslims, caste Sikhs and so on in this society.

The concluding chapter takes up the major thematic concerns of the previous chapters and attempts a cognitive and summative evaluation of the ideas presented and lists out the major arguments and implications of the study. The material and historical reality of the experience of hegemony and marginalization on caste and gender lines that is continuing and worsening in the present would be taken up in detail. Questions of class analytical perspectives in the context of Brahmanic patriarchy would be explicated and critiqued. The need for a subaltern hermeneutics and the urgency of epistemological democratization would also be discussed as a political and emancipatory outcome of the study in conclusion.

Notes

1. For an early analysis of sociality in the fictional narrative in India see Meenakshi Mukherjee, *Realism and Reality:*

The Novel and Society in India (New Delhi: Oxford UP, 1985). Also see Raymond Williams, "Forms of English Fiction in 1848," *Literature, Politics and Theory,* eds. Francis Barker, et al. (London: Methuen, 1986) 1-16; also see his *The English Novel from Dickens to Lawrence* (London: Hogarth, 1985).

2. Andrew Gibson, *Postmodernity, Ethics and the Novel: From Leavis to Levinas* (London: Routledge, 1999).
3. Michel Foucault, *The Order of Things: An Archaeology of the Human Sciences* (New York: Vintage, 1994) 46-48.
4. Jacques Derrida, *The Truth in Painting,* trans. Geoff Bennington and Ian MacLeod. (London: U of Chicago P, 1987) 6.
5. "Discourse" is used in the Foucauldian sense of language practice or language in social praxis that implies power relationships intervening in practices of representation. See Michel Foucault, *The Order of Things* (New York: Vintage, 1994) 79-81.
6. Raymond Williams and Edward Said, *The Politics of Modernism: Against the New Conformists* (London: Verso, 1989) 177-97.
7. Gayatri Spivak, *In Other Worlds: Essays in Cultural Politics* (NewYork: Routledge, 1988) 103-17. See particularly the chapter "Explanation and Culture: Marginalia."
8. For an elaboration of the notion of narrativity and textuality of history, see Keith Jenkins, *Why History: Ethics and Postmodernity* (London: Routledge, 1998) and for a discussion of the margins of national and narrative discourses, see Homi Bhabha, "Dissemination: Time, Narrative and the Margins of the Modern Nation" in *Nation and Narration,* ed. Homi Bhabha (London: Routledge, 1990) 291-322.
9. Susan Bayly, *Caste, Society and Politics in India from the 18th c. to the Modern Age* (Cambridge: Cambridge UP, 1999); Ghanashyam Shah, *Caste and Democratic Politics in India* (New Delhi: Permanent Black, 2003).

For a Hindu hermeneutics of this Brahmanic treaty, see M K Gandhi, *Varnasramadharma* (Bombay: Navjivan, 1962).

10. The conceptual category of "Dalit Bahujan" carries all the socio cultural and political significations employed in its development and use in Gopal Guru ("dalitbahujan"), Gail Omvedt ("dalit bahujan") and Kancha Ilaiah, as well as in the dalitbahujan feminists. The use of the word by political leaders like Kanshi Ram and Mayawati can also be considered in this regard.

11. V Geetha and S V Rajadurai, "Neo Brahmanism: An Intentional Fallacy?" *Economic and Political Weekly* 28 (1993): 129-36; Uma Chakravarty, "Saffronising the Past: Of Myths, Histories and Right Wing Agendas," *Economic and Political Weekly* 33 (1998): 225-32; Sumit Sarkar, "The Fascism of the Sangh Parivar," *Economic and Political Weekly* 28 (1993): 163-67; and Satish Deshpande, "Communalising the Nation-space: Notes on Spatial Strategies of Hindutva," *Economic and Political Weekly* 30 (1995): 3220-3227.

12. For details of historical and institutional inequality in India under caste hegemony, see K L Sharma, *Social Inequality in India: Profiles of Caste, Class and Social Mobility* (New Delhi: Rawat, 2001) and for the problematic of historical epistemological conflict, see Kancha Ilaiah, "Brahmanism Vs Dalitism: The Epistemological Conflict in History," *Cultural Subordination and the Dalit Challenge: Dalit identity and Politics,* ed. Ghanshyam Shah (New Delhi: Sage, 2001) 108-28.

13. Niraja Gopal Jayal, ed., *Democracy in India* (New Delhi: Oxford UP, 2001), specifically the essay by Omvedt, "The Anti Caste Movement and the Discourse of Power" (481-508).

14. Partha Chatterjee, "Caste and Subaltern Consciousness," *Subaltern Studies VI,* ed. Ranajit Guha (New Delhi: Oxford UP, 1989) 169-209.

15. D D Kosambi, *Combined Methods in Indology and Other Writings: D D Kosambi*, ed. B Chathopadhyaya (New Delhi: Oxford UP, 2002) 87-97. For a detailed theoretical analysis of the hierarchical ideology of Brahmanism see Louis Dumont, *Homo Hierarchicus: The Caste System and Its Implications*. London: Paladin, 1970.
16. See Susan Bayly, *Caste, Society and Politics in India from the 18th c. to the Modern Age*.
17. For a historical trajectory of Anti Brahmanic, Anti caste movements in India, see Gail Omvedt, *Dalit Visions: The Anti Caste Movements and the Construction of an Indian Identity* (New Delhi: Orient Longman, 1995). Also see her *Dalit and Democratic Revolution: Dr Ambedkar and the Dalit Movement in Colonial India* (New Delhi: Sage, 1994) and *Buddhism in India: Challenging Brahmanism and Caste* (New Delhi: Sage, 2005). For a subaltern hermeneutics of Buddhism, see B R Ambedkar, *The Buddha and his Dhamma* (Bombay: SCP, 1957) and G P Deshpande, "Metaphysics and Protest in Discourse on Buddhism," *Economic and Political Weekly* 39 (2004): 3109-10. For Phule's contestations of Brahmanic nationalism see Rosalind O'Hanlon, *Caste, Conflict and Ideology: Mahatma Jotiba Phule and low Caste Social Protest in 19th c. Western India* (Cambridge: Cambridge UP, 1988).
18. On this, see Gayatri Spivak, "Subaltern Studies: Deconstructing Historiography," *Subaltern Studies IV*, ed. Ranajit Guha (New Delhi: Oxford UP, 1985) 338-63; "Can the Subaltern Speak?," *Marxism and the Interpretation of Culture*, ed. Cary Nelson and Lawrence Grossberg (Urbana: U of Illinois P, 1988) 51-88; "On the New Subaltern," *Subaltern Studies XI*, ed. Partha Chatterjee and Pradeep Jagannathan (New Delhi: Permanent Black, 2000) 305-34. Also see Rudolf C. Heredia, "Subaltern Alternatives on Caste, Class and Ethnicity," *Contributions to Indian Sociology* 34. 1 (2000): 37-62 which points towards a subaltern hermeneutics and Dalitization of culture and polity.

19. See Partha Chatterjee, *The Nation and its Fragments: Colonial and Post Colonial Histories* (New Delhi: Oxford UP, 1994), specifically the chapters: "Whose Imagined Community," "The Nationalist Elite," "The Nation and its Outcastes" and "Communities and the Nation."
20. Christophe Jaffrelot, *India's Silent Revolution: The Rise of the Low Castes in North Indian Politics* (New Delhi: Permanent Black, 2003).
21. Asgar Ali Engineer, ed., *Mandal Commission Controversy* (Delhi: Ajanta, 1991) specifically Gail Omvedt, "Twice Born Riot Against Democracy" (6-25).
22. Gopal Guru, "Understanding Ambedkar's Construction of National Movement," *Economic and Political Weekly* 33 (1998): 156-57, identifies the social thrust of Ambedkar's nationalism as against the political thrust of the "unified - nation" theory of the Hindu Brahmanic nationalists.
23. Bipan Chandra, "Reservations and Development" (164-70) and Omvedt, "Twice Born Riots against Democracy" (6-25) in Engineer, *Mandal Commission Controversy*.
24. For a critique of community and communitization, see Jean Luc Nancy, *Inoperative Community* (Minneapolis: U of Minnesota P, 1991) and David Rasmussen, ed., *Universalism vs. Communitarianism* (Cambridge: MIT P, 1992).
25. See Gopal Guru, "How Egalitarian are the Social Sciences in India?," *Economic and Political Weekly* 37 (2002): 5003-09 for a brilliant analysis of the "epistemological imperialism" of the academy and of the social science practices in India by the TTB (top twice born). For a comprehensive survey of the material manifestation of caste hierarchy and hegemony throughout Indian public sphere and state apparatuses, see Andre Beteille, *Equality and Universality: Essays in Social and Political Theory* (New Delhi: Oxford UP, 2002) 178-86.
26. Uma Chakravarty, "Conceptualising Brahmanic Patriarchy in Early India: Caste, Gender, Class and

State," *Economic and Political Weekly* 28 (1993): 579-85; "Reconceptualising Gender: Phule, Brahmanism and Brahmanical Patriarchy" in Anupama Rao (164-79), *Gender and Caste*. Also Leela Dube, "Caste and Women "(223-48) in the same volume.

27. See Spivak, "Can the Subaltern Speak?"
28. Susie Tharu and Satish Poduval, "Refiguring Literary/ Cultural Historiography," *Economic and Political Weekly* 33 (1998): 1508-09 theorizes this erosion of boundaries in the discourse of the human sciences in India.
29. Anupama Rao, *Gender and Caste* (New Delhi: Kali for Women, 2003) 1-47.
30. Kumkum Sangari and Uma Chakravarty, eds., *From Myth to Markets: Essays on Gender* (New Delhi: Manohar and IIAS, 2001); Vasantha Kannabiran and Kalpana Kannabiran, "Caste and Gender: Understanding Dynamics of Power and Violence," *Economic and Political Weekly* 26 (1991): 2130-33.
31. Susie Tharu, "The Impossible Subject: Caste and the Gendered Body," *Economic and Political Weekly* 31(1996): 1311-15; Susie Tharu and T Niranjana, "Problems of a Contemporary Theory of Gender," *Social Scientist* 22 (1994): 232-36.
32. Besides Anupama Rao above, also see Gopal Guru, "Dalit Women Talk Differently" (80-85) in the same volume and Vrinda Nabar, *Caste as Women* (New Delhi: Penguin, 1995).
33. Antonio Gramsci, *Selections from Prison Notebooks*, ed. and trans. Quintin Hoare and G N Smith (New York: International Publishers, 1971) 12. Gramsci sees hegemony as the power that "the dominant group exercises through out society" in contradistinction to "direct domination or command exercised through the state and juridical government." Regarding the subaltern he adds, "the subaltern classes by definition, are not united and can not unite until they are able to become a 'state'... the history of the subaltern groups is fragmented and episodic. There undoubtedly does exist

a tendency to unification in the historical activity of these groups...continually interrupted by the activity of the ruling groups...even when they appear triumphant the subaltern groups are merely anxious to defend themselves" (52, 54-55).

34. This notion of the dialectics of modernity is developed from P P Raveendran, *Indian Literature: Readings from the Margin* (Forthcoming) 5-17.

1

Caste in Religion : *Godan, Song of the Loom*

> It is god who creates the high and the low. One comes into wealth after a lot of penance. It is the fruit of the deeds of our past life. We sowed nothing and we have nothing to reap. *(Godan* 18)

> There were groups within groups, like the numerous strands unravelled from a single, partially coloured silken thread. (*Song of the Loom* 5)

Recent scholarship identifies Premchand as the first Hindi/Urdu writer to take up the Dalit Bahujan question as part of an explicit political agenda. Shashi Bhooshan Upadhyay says he was the first to portray the Dalits as independent and recognizable characters both as part of the poor and with their own particular problems. Meenakshi Mukherjee also contextualizes the text of *Godan* in its conflict ridden times.[1]

The marginalia represented in *Godan* is that of the north Indian peasantry with its caste and gender attributes. It is a representation of the segment of the Indian society that becomes the base of the social and economic fabric of the nation, according to subaltern historians like Partha Chatterjee.[2] The narrative is set in the casteist, feudal and Brahman centred Hindi/Urdu village of Uttar Pradesh and the title itself shows the central motif; the giving in charity of a cow to a Brahman. The peasant family of Hori Ram, his wife Dhania and son Gobar collapse in their struggle to own a cow and then to give another in charity to the Brahman.

The images of the cow and the Brahman are therefore as central to the narrative as is the culture it tries to represent and narrativize. This foregrounds the central characteristics of the ideology of Brahmanism and its material manifestation in Hinduism.[3] The holy cow and the holy Brahman, the protection of which is proclaimed as the supreme duty of every Hindu, especially the Shudra, and valourized as one of the Sanatana Dharmas is a typical obscurantist dogma that perpetuated the Brahmanic hegemony.

This sacred supremacy of the cow over other milk-giving mammals like the buffalo and that of the Brahman over the Bahujan has been constructed and maintained in and through a range of metaphysical texts and social discourses and practices including those of purity and pollution. The cow and Brahman become sacred through divine and sacred origins; while the cow is a descendent of the heavenly Kamadhenu, the paradisiacal archetypal mammal capable of giving anything, Brahman, the Bhudeva is a direct earthly incarnation of the gods. Both are objects of desire whose sanctity and purity are unquestionable and unsurpassable. This supremacy is further established in contrast and comparison, through the construction of "others" and opposites. While the cow is normally light skinned and mild, the buffalo is dark and rough. While the Brahman is "fairer and clean" the Bahujan is less so, and so on and so forth![4]

This othering and stratification is also complicated through beastly associations attributed to the Bahujan. Thus the killing of the cow and Brahman are the supreme offences and the gifting of a cow, especially to its suitable counterpart, the Brahman is a supreme act of virtue that pleases the gods. These are some of the premises under which the Bahujans and Muslims who work in the meat and leather industry have been historically imagined and marked as others and evil incarnates. And it is the same sentimentality and governmentality that skirts around the sacred cow-Brahman nexus that the Hindu nationalists are utilizing in making cow slaughter a poll issue.[5]

This is the historical and cultural context in which we situate the infatuation of the peasantry for owning the cow and giving it away in charity to a Brahman, as enacted in the story of Hori in the narrative. Though they are the backbone of India's economic production these peasants have always been outsiders to the system, condemned to live in material and cultural margins due to the discursive contexts explained earlier. In the Belari village of Uttar Pradesh, Hori Ram and his wife Dhania, their son Gobardhan and daughters Sona and Rupa were struggling it out in a caste feudal system that indebted them and reduced them to mere bonded labour. In the words of Hori:

> It is all due to keeping on good terms with the *master* that trouble has remained at arm's length from us. Otherwise we would have been wiped out of existence long ago. Out of scores of people in the village can you name one who has not been ejected from his land or been served with attachment orders? When your neck is being trampled under the *tyrant's heel* the safest course is *to keep on tickling* his feet. (5)

The subaltern peasantry, both men and women are enmeshed in this barbaric power structure that assumes fierce proportions in its mix-up with caste, Varna and Brahmanism. The feudal lord rules the village with an iron fist. See how the narrative has it: "Digvijay Singh, educated, but vain, heartless, tightfisted, *chased low caste women of the villag*e and kept disgusting company" (260). But the woman has some sense of justice to question the system of the Zamindari, the reign of the feudal caste lord:

> But Dhania was not so well up in worldly matters, she thought that at the most what the Zamindar could claim was the rent in exchange for tilling his land. Then why play the sycophant? Why should one touch the soles of a Zamindar's feet? To be sure, during the twenty years of her married life she had fully realized that even if she lived a niggardly life stinted on food and clothes scraped

together every elusive anna, it was difficult to liquidate the rent of the Zamindar. But even then she would not admit defeat. On this matter the husband and wife had differences every now and then.(5)

This is the penury they are fated to live in, and the struggle against the odds is visible in the woman and in the husband in different ways. For Hori the possession of a cow is a mark of his privileged social status. The significance of the cow as symbolic capital has been dealt with. The cow assumes this symbolic and iconic relevance in relation to the signifying systems and discourses of Brahmanism. It has its material links to the Varna and caste system as well as to the systems of language and culture. As the marker of his social status as a 'worthy householder' in the village, it signifies his Brahmanical connection and assimilated 'culture':

> *Not a cow of native* breed, Oh those were no good. Their yield of milk was poor and their calves good for nothing. Only fit to be yoked to an oil expeller. He had set his heart on a *foreign pedigreed cow*. He would swamp her with care. She would yield plentiful milk [..] the cow of course would not cost less than two hundred rupees. What did it matter? Didn't a cow tied by the door enhance the *prestige of the house*? And how *auspicious to see* a cow the first thing in the morning! (7)

The emphases clearly show the romanticized/mythicized obscurantist discourse that makes the cow an obscure object of desire, connected with the high culture of Brahmanism. See the contempt for the native breeds and the longing for the foreign cattle. The privileging of the non-native over the native in the discourse that does the legitimizing and canonizing function for the Sanskritized Brahmanic etiquette of 'auspiciousness' and social 'prestige' is to be taken note of. "Like every householder Hori for a long time had been cherishing this desire for the cow. It was the brightest dream of his life, his greatest ambition" (7).

Thus to become a 'householder' you need to own a cow, not a goat or buffalo. Though Hori manages to get a cow from Bhola, a neighbour, his jealous brother Hira poisons it. This fact again indicates how precious and cherished an object is the cow in the popular imagination. The arrival of the cow itself was uplifting for the simple folk: "With the cow's arrival a great change came over Dhania: proud she talked of nothing but the animal" (75). Also note the "change" at its death:

> Dhania beat her head in despair. Hori ran to fetch Pandit Datadin, the self appointed veterinary of the village. The news ran through the village and people collected at Hori's door. The cow it was evident had been poisoned. Poisoning the sacred cow! It was unheard of! Everyone was stunned. Hira most of all. He fumed with rage, threatening to hack the beastly culprit to pieces if he could lay his hands on him.(79)

To intensify the emotional tension of the narrative the discourse changes from the mimetic to the dialogic at this moment. It also registers the cosmic effect of this most heinous act that is culturally specific: "The village lay in darkness; the cow dead and at a distance of ten feet from her, Hori tossing on his cot. Only the belt round the bullock's necks tinkled now and then. Hori's gloom seemed to make the night darker" (80).

Gobar falls in love with Jhunia, the widowed young daughter of Bhola. She becomes pregnant and is given asylum by Hori and Dhania, as Gobar goes to the city for work. This leads to the ostracism of the family by the village worthies. A fine is also imposed on them. The infuriated Bhola also walks away with Hori's pair of bullocks. Hori works as a common labourer in other fields. He is also submerged in debt that keeps on increasing at alarming rates of interest. Even Gobar refuses to help since he could not agree with the old man's fatalistic affiliations. Towards the end of his life Hori works hard as a coolie by day and a weaver by night to make money for buying a cow, and to feed his grandchild. But he perishes in the heat and escapes the problems of the family. Dhania also tries to give a cow in charity to a Brahman. She does not succeed in it and when the Brahman comes the old woman also breathes her last by confessing that there is neither cow nor money in the house.

Not only obscurantist and hegemonic discourses like those of purity and pollution, previous births and Karma, and of divine sanctions and supremacy, but ritual also plays a very important role in the sustenance of caste-Hindu village societies. The narrative also depicts this aspect:

> For six months in twelve, you can hear drums and cymbals celebrating one festival or the other [..] the village of Semari is no exception. The threat of the money lenders and the oppression of the underlings of the Zamindars cannot curb the villager's zest. It matters little if the peasant starves or has no shirt on his back and no money in his pocket. (172-3)

These village festivals are the seminal sites which ensure the reestablishment of a sense of hierarchy and institutionalized inequality through their caste-feudal loyalties and ritual relations. Though some critics are of the opinion that the city episodes of Rai Sahib and the Mehta-Malti accounts provide a contrast to this rural primitivism, it is also an extension of the caste Swaraj. The Hindu city as the Hindu village is ruled over by family names and caste supremacy discourses.[6]

Another item of the symbolic capital that ties down the subaltern peasantry is land. It is another source of prestige in the village and is as important as the cow and the Brahmanic connection. See the dispute between Hori and his progressive-minded son Gobar, who is critical of the traditional practices of the villagers, and prefers a city life:

> It is no use arguing with you my son, Hori said. 'Does anybody ever give up his *ancestral property*? Look at us

for instance. What do we get out of our land? ... But we don't give up our land and go in for a job. Do we? Our *prestige* gets in the way. Well that is exactly the case with the Zamindar.'(17)

Ancestral property is also considered sacred in the religious sense as ancestral occupation, something that sustains the occupational underpinning of caste. The questioning younger generation is taught that the inequality and the hierarchy are god given, religious and natural:

'So do you think there is no difference between him and us?' 'None. God has made us all equal.' 'That is not true son; it is god who creates the high and the low. One comes into wealth after a lot of penance. It is the fruit of the deeds of our past life. We sowed nothing and we have nothing to reap.' 'These are only fancies that console the mind. God has created us all equal. Those who have power oppress the poor and become rich.' (18)

This sense of guilt in the past life and the Karma theory has been central in subordinating the masses as Shudras and Avarnas under caste Hinduism. The instinct for equality is aborted in birth itself through religious sentiments and meta-spiritual fantasies. To counter the challenge of Buddhism, the eighth century Brahmanic ideologue Sankara propagated the Karma and Maya theories among the masses throughout the peninsula. For this hegemonic pedagogic practice he established Brahmanic Maths all over the peninsula. He is widely known as Prachanna Buddha for his cunning appropriation of the Buddha's Sunyavada into Hindu/Brahmanic Mayavada and Advaita.[7] According to critics like J Reghu, Advaita is a rejection of the other and an assertion of the empire of the Self.[8] Since there is nothing beyond the One, and since the other is impossible in the unending oneness, ethics and politics are also impossible in this totalizing order of the self. Here ethics is understood as the unconditional acknowledgment of the existence of the other. This empire of the eternal Sovereign

Self was the prototype of late nineteenth century cultural nationalist avatars of Hindu revivalism, the recent resurgences of the unending trajectory of Brahmanic Hindu colonialism. See the articulations and operations of the same self-centred, supremacist discourse in Datadin's voice, which entangles the peasant in eternal debt and doubling interest rates:

> 'Son, *I am a Brahman*, you wont live in peace by devouring my money. I am a Brahman and I know how to get back my money. You will come to my doors and offer me the money on bent knees.' Gobar was unperturbed. But a storm raged in Hori's mind. Had it been a Thakur's or Bania's money it wouldn't have mattered. But a *Brahman's money*! God keep him from a *Brahman's wrath*. They said *if a Brahman's wrath visited a person* not a single member in the family survived. Hori's religious sentiments tugged at his mind. He ran and fell at Datadin's feet. '*Maharaj* as long as I live I will see that I pay back every piece of your debt. Pay no heed to what my son has said. This matter is between you and me. He can't interfere.'(176)

This social and 'spiritual' subordination is followed by the subaltern's physical and even bodily invasion by Brahmanism. The historic construction of sexual colonies among Shudra women by Brahmans was a complete conquest of the bodies and minds. The Brahmanic patriarchy wants to master the subaltern woman's sexuality, which can be potentially subversive to the masculine discourses of Brahmanism: "that a low caste woman should be so haughty was too much for Pateshwari" (217). Though the low castes are polluting by touch and sometimes by sight, the high priests of Brahmanism could well manage to sleep with the subaltern woman. Not just money but the beauty of the subaltern woman too is an offering to the Brahman, as Jhunia tells Gobar. Look at the way Datadin, the temple priest, seduces the low caste women of the village:

'What will you reply when god asks: I gave you so much beauty and you didn't even look kindly at a Brahman. Speak up. I am a Brahman thirsting for a word from your lips. I get money in alms everyday it is your beauty's alms that I crave for today.' (38)

The same is the story of Matadin, the priest's prodigy who seduces a Chamar girl named Selia. The Brahman sleeps with her but refuses the food she touches. The 'purity' is retained through early morning baths and associated rituals. It goes to such an extent that finally the Chamar folk had to make him a Chamar by pushing down a bone under his throat. How he got his 'purity' back is more revealing:

> After spending a couple of hundred rupees on the Pandits of Banaras, Matadin had again been declared a Brahman and taken back into the fold. That day a big yajya was performed, scores of Brahmans feasted, many mantras chanted as part of the purification ceremony, Matadin had to taste cow dung and cow's urine; the cow dung purified his heart and the urine killed the pernicious bacteria of defilement that had got lodged in his soul. (273)

The narrative foregrounds the riddles of purity and pollution and the ritualistic dogma of Brahmanism with a reformist zeal and suggests an alternative movement that appears a little too down-to-earth for the high priests:

> Well the penance did really purify him. From that day he developed a revulsion for dharma, and dumped his priesthood in the Ganga. For he realized that although his patrons still asked him to work out auspicious dates and consulted him in matters of marriage and births. They refused water from his hands and did not allow him to touch their utensils: in spite of the fact that the Pandit in Banaras have accepted him as a Brahman. In disgust he turned a tiller of the soil. (273)

He ends up in Selia's hut, confessing that he will worship her and that her hut is his temple. He says he wants to become a cobbler, but still he has this binary of the Brahman/cobbler in his discourse, reminding us of Praneshacharya in *Samskara* (see the third chapter), who even after the whole ordeal reduces the Bahujan culture as a mere cockfight. Matadin has it this way: "all those who fulfill their dharma are Brahman, and all those who violate their dharma are cobblers" (275).

This points towards a general pattern obtaining in the Indian fictional narratives. While narrativizing the tension between the two epistemologies of Brahmanism and Bahujan culture, even works that appear to resist hegemonic discourses end up reasserting the existing power relations. This is indicated by the novel *Gramayana* also that reestablishes the master-slave relationship at the concluding part. We feel the same frustrated sense of the unchangeability of the social hierarchy and hegemony in *The God of Small Things* too in the end. A domestic and personal reconciliation is suggested in *Thalamurakal* that takes up the greater questions of race and ethnicity. Such a general pattern points towards the inadequacy of the fictional discourse in confronting power and the intrinsic limitations of the narrative medium that fails to subvert hegemony. The cultural and artistic character of the genre's ideology that neutralizes radicalism is also brought into the limelight. The formalistic/artistic/literary elements of the genre have their traditional and cultural affiliations with the prevalent tastes, worldviews and hegemonic ideology. But what is interesting is that again and again these narrative works bring to light the inevitable questions of caste, Brahmanism and social inequality that operate across religious cultures.

The religious minorities in India have always been outside the imagined nation space and the hegemonic cultural nationalist discourses monopolized and propagated by the elitist Hindu worldview.[9] The history and politics of partition and the Mandir-Masjid politics and pogroms that followed in the last few decades orchestrated by the cultural nationalist forces have only helped to consolidate their cultural alienation and 'othering.'[10] As the single largest minority group that could slightly threaten, at least in the Hindi/Urdu belt, the pseudo-majoritarian ideology of Hindutva and present an alternative religion for the Bahujan masses, Muslims have been the specific targets of this fascist rightwing propaganda in post-independence India.[11] From the time of the origin of cultural nationalism in nineteenth century Bengal renaissance, Muslims were at the receiving end of the symbolic violence appearing in the nationalist discourses, and this continues in the popular cinema, in television serials and in media representations.[12] The atrocities are not confined to symbolic and metaphorically hegemonic violence, but are perpetrated at the material, racial and ethnic levels leading to holocausts.[13] Almost all of the post-independence riots and pogroms have resulted in Muslim casualties.[14] The 1984 Delhi genocide exterminated five thousand Sikhs and the 2002 Gujarat massacre witnessed the organized annihilation of thousands of Muslims.[15] Thus it is not just the Dalit Bahujans or the 'Mlechas' who come under attack from the forces of Indian fascism, but the religious minorities as well, especially Muslims, Sikhs and Christians.[16]

This context of symbolic and actual massacre as well as the cultural erasure and purging of the collective unconscious as a consent-manufacturing process problematizes any attempt at the ethico-political representation of the minority marginalia in India.[17] *Song of the Loom* (1996), a fictional narrative attempt at representing the life of Muslim weavers, women, men and children who struggle for their livelihood in Banaras, assumes significance here. This Urdu novel by Abdul Bismillah which takes its original title *Jhini Jhini Bini Chadariya* from poet Kabir who was also a master weaver of Banaras, portrays the hard toil of the community of Ansaris in and around this old North Indian city along the Ganges which is a sacred and central spot in the cultural geography of the Hindu imagiNation: "Banaras or Kashi is said to be the oldest city in the world" (Prologue).[18] The location is significant as Banaras/Kasi is at the centre of the Brahmanical nation space, on whose margins reside the 'Mlechas' the others of the Brahmanic purity and pollution.[19]

The story is simple and concerns the daily struggle for existence carried out by Mateen, a poor weaver of the renowned Banaras silk saris, and his ailing wife Aleemun, who could never afford to wear a single silk sari woven by her husband. "They were master craftsmen who wrought such wonders from silk to adorn the elite, the privileged, the makers of History" (Prologue).[20] The weavers' struggle to get a just remuneration and their efforts at escaping the shackles of the middlemen and exploiters are narrativized with subtlety and detail in the novel. One might see parallels between the intricate and vivid composition, a product of fictional weaving, and the art of silk weaving that forms the theme of the novel. Here we see how the message of working culture shapes the medium in subtle but suggestively political ways.

The subversive political potential of representation does not end with this form-theme merging narration that focuses on working people and their culture. The narrative also exposes the vividness of the imagined, homogenized "other" peoples and communities. It etches the community as a plural and polyphonic formation. It also explodes the myth of "anti national and traitorous" minority pressure groups. It depicts the deep cleavages of class, caste and gender inequities and tensions within this marginalia of the imagined other community.[21] It also problematizes the gendered and "new subaltern" identities from within the periphery of this marginalia.[22]

Aleemun, the consumption-stricken wife of Mateen, is a representation of the erased existence of woman in this marginal and subaltern Mohallah. This ailing woman in the veil foregrounds the hidden patriarchy within the subaltern:

> Aleemun had consumption. Mateen was painfully aware of this, but he could do nothing about it. A wife must attend to the household chores. The sorting, spinning and winding of yarn, the cooking, cleaning and washing- she had to do all this. There was no getting away from this. She had to remain in purdah too. She couldn't go out in the open for fresh air, could she? The laws of society were absolute. It was a sin to violate them. Mateen knew this. From Chittanpura to Madanpura these laws were uniformly observed. The people living here were the followers of the Holy Prophet. They were Ansaris the descendants of Hazrat Ayub Anssari, who had given refuge to his holy presence, the prophet. Mateen had grown up with this knowledge, but whether it was true he did not know. He did however abide by the laws. As did others. (4)

The domestic diversity and caste hangover is astonishing within this community of weavers and Muslims as a larger community. This could be situated within the Indian social reality of hierarchy and stratification in the historical context of Brahmanism and its Varna-caste ideology, that has contaminated all religious cultures. It also brings to the forefront the question of caste in conversion and that of the Dalit Bahujan Muslims.

> In a way the entire world constitute a single community. Within it there is another community known as India. Within India too, the Hindus have their own community. The Muslims their own. And then there is the Jolaha community of Banaras in which there are many divisions: Paancho (The Five), Chaudaho (The Fourteen), Baisi (The Twenty two), and Bavano (The Fifty two). There was even a new Baisi, now. Each group had its own elder, its own chief. But the elder of Paancho was considered supreme [..] there were groups within groups, like the numerous strands unraveled from a single, partially colored silken thread. (4-5)

These sub-caste groups were often at loggerheads with each other and were engaged in bloody feuds. This is apart from the Shia – Sunni divide that is almost universal among Muslisms (219). Each group as in the Brahmanical sub-castes claimed antiquity, purity, ethnic superiority and cultural supremacy. The all-pervasive and hegemonic potential of the Brahmanical racist ideology could again be seen here:

> Preparations were on since morning. Preparations! Not only for the Friday Namaz, but also for the clash. The original Baisi and the new one were at loggerheads. The dispute was about the maidan where the namaz was to be offered. That was all. And it had started with the formation of the new Baisi. (29)

Discontent, dissent and all kinds of regressions and escapisms that complicate the chaos of the margin are common among the male folk, who are squeezed to the core by the middlemen:

> Those who don't want to be seen committing a sin approached the palm grove under cover of the dusky shadows of the evening. Holding a corner of their lungis, with one hand, wearing skull caps, engrossed in talking about Allah and his prophet, singing the praises of Pakistan and heaping abuses on Hindustan, these people wandered like cranes into the grove by evening. (9)

Internal class exploitation of craftsmen and workers by rich merchants and middlemen are enacted in the Mateen – Ameerullah episode:

> Mateen's heart sank at Haaji saheb's words. He failed to understand how Haji sahib unfailingly managed to find flows in each sari. Either the tension was too great, or it was too long. Or the pattern was unduly bold [..] the colour was not right [..] the silk had been spun too thin [..] the list was endless. And that was that - take it or leave it. (14)

The struggle and toil of the weaver is 'immortalized' here in a certain celebratory and romanticizing way with an echo of Kabir, the weaver-poet. But apart from making a faint reference to the saintly aspects of Kabir's personality, the text makes no mention of the radical content and subversive aspect of Kabir's poetry.

> Rauf uncle was busy weaving. His aged body propped behind the loom looked exactly like the picture of Kabir in books. Mateen had seen the illustration in his class five book. Rauf uncle wore only a lungi and there was a skull cap on his head. He had taken off his shirt which lay beside him. There was a purple sari on the loom. Golden thread was coiled on the nari and silken thread on the dhota – as if the sun and moon were shining together in the sky as the loom of the universe moved in an incessant rhythm [..]. (28)

See the cosmic invocation of the heavenly bodies and the universal character of the romantic myth employed. The metaphoric narration takes a metaphysical turn here. This is one plane where the text defeats its own attempt to represent and articulate the subaltern voice and the marginal material reality. It also shares the fate of Kabir as a cult figure and a canonical poet, whose Dohas or Verses are now subjected celebrated through canonization and academic appropriation.

This hegemonic appropriation could again be seen signified in the Hindu hegemonic influence on the local Muslim festivals and customs. Divali and Karthik that encode historic, symbolic, genocidal racism and anti-other violence manufacture consent and support from the targets and preys themselves. It provides us the space to rethink about the shocking fact that all Hindu festivals celebrating the victory of the godly races against the uncultured others are getting wide currency and legitimacy among the Bahujan masses for whose ideological and symbolic subordination these were devised in the first place. For a superb example take for instance Onam the national festival of Kerala, which celebrates the end of Bali-Raj and the victory by cheat of disguised Brahmanism in the form of the dwarf with a sacred thread, Lord Vamana who is even worshipped as a deity in a Savarna temple in central Kerala in Thrikakara. What the above example suggests is that public discourses and semiotics are burdened with images and signs of the dominant discourse and could assume hegemonic proportions in a very 'normal' way.

> This year at Diwali Haji Ameerullah had distributed one kilo packs of sweets to his artisans. Previously it used to be half a kilo. Not even on the last Wednesday had they ever got a one kilo pack [..] the Hindu artisans came from the village got an extra half kilo pack each. (27-8)

These festivals were also sites of contestation and conflict, time for bloody negotiations of old rivalries and feuds;

> Holi went by safely without incident. The question of safety or otherwise hung over this festival because any Hindu child could accidentally throw colour on a Muslim brother [..] even such a small incident, though, could easily take an ugly turn. (44)

Another typical instance of the romanticization of the weaver community's misery could be seen in the hyperbolic analogy of a Tabla player. As mentioned above in the early part of the novel there are many cosmic and clichéd images that help to elevate the material misery as noble and uplifting:

> Like a tabla player, who first taps the tabla to adjust its tautness, then tries it out for tone and finally begins the accompaniment to the song. So too the cadence of music and design emerging in the texture of the sari fused with the consciousness of the artist at one point till it vanished altogether. (51-2)

But the representation of woman is more radical and subversive. The real margin within the margin is lighted up to reveal the veiled victims in the Purdah, the victims of subaltern patriarchy.[23]

> Lateef had divorced Kamrun. When Aleemun gave this news to Mateen he was not surprised. Divorce had become quite common in the community. What was the status of a woman, after all? [...] To be kicked in the ass and thrown out whenever the husband wanted. That was the way to deal with a woman. Wasn't it? She was there to spin, cook, clean and to sleep with her husband, bear his children and look after his needs. If she demurred in doing any of these, he could follow the laws of Islam and pronounce the verdict of divorce on her [..] 'Talaq! Talaq! Talaq!' (56)

As Hindu festivals and rituals are hegemonic and all-pervasive so are acts of black magic and witch craft. Hindu gods, demons and their keepers and exorcists also transgress religious boundaries.[24] The Bahujans in particular are the historic victims of such occult practices. Exorcism and purification also target and exploit women sexually and psychologically (see for instance Rehana's story, 74). Significantly, it is always women who are possessed, and termed as "possessed women" (84).

The narrative represents not just the work culture of the Bahujans in the periphery but their food culture too. The toiling masses depend upon locally available and relatively cheap beef as their chief delicacy and the main source of energy. Mutton and other varieties of meat are too expensive and are rare delights (89). Such representations of the food habits, rights and work culture of the Bahujans have immense political relevance and should be contextualized in the "anti-slaughter" and "sacred cow" discourse deliberately manufactured by the Hindu right.[25] But interestingly the narrative balances this with another description about the decaying slaughter leftover lying around after the festive seasons are over (110).

The reference here is definitely to the decaying margins too, that struggle to survive on rotten meat, invoked throughout the narrative. Mateen at his best could ever hope for a leftover-breakfast. Cheap meat, obviously rotten is the daily intake, that couldn't even slightly support in the daily toil at the loom and in the open. All men and women, not to mention children and the old, are under-nourished. This itself is the chief cause of infant mortality and ill health among the Bahujans.

Elitist and cultural monopoly claims are part of almost all communities in the Brahmanical society. Muslim Bahujans are not an exception. "Haji" which means one who has visited Mecca is a title with a lot of symbolic capital attached to it. But the astonishing fact is that even among Hajis there are specific caste demarcations. They themselves are the most privileged, among Muslims, but they too have their internal hierarchy which is a leftover of the ancient Brahmanical caste-tags. In the novel they even have a cobbler Haji, "Haji Chamar" (99).

Self-mutilation is an age-old penance of Bahujans in the Brahmanical society and an indication of their masculinity, virility, loyalty and ultimately the symbolic acceptance of Brahmanic hegemony. The simultaneous presence of an element of self-contempt and a seemingly subversive sacrificial element makes this peculiar expression contradictory. This paradox is characteristic of the subaltern ritualistic performances in the subcontinent, especially in the south. For example, in Kerala there are practices of fire-walking and claw-hanging, which are celebrated as expressions of "subaltern speech and resistance" and are revived in parts of the region with the active involvement of the Hindu rightwing organizations. Such expressions of self-mutilation are often treated as symbolic of one's religious commitment and affiliation. It is also practiced in Arabia and west Asia, and the self-mutilation of Ansaris, represented in the novel, does belong to this category. The young men in procession beat their breasts violently to show their devotion and submission to the god and the sect, and in material terms to the priestly elders (118).

An alternative way and culture to this hegemonic influence of Brahmanism is also suggested briefly by the narrative at the point where Mateen travels, in search of work outside Banaras to Saranath, where the Buddha delivered his first sermon.[26] In the railway station he reads "haltingly, picking out each word" about the Buddha and his Dharma (133).

The minorities are generally afraid of the nationalist governments as well as the state and its apparatuses. That is why the politics of family planning and the related demographic discourses become sites of suspicion and terror for the voiceless and the victims of history. The "breeding other," the "hoggish" subaltern woman, the "Mlecha Yoni" in classical Brahmanic terms, is perceived as an all time deadly threat to monopoly groups. It subverts their nationalist and pseudo-majoritarian dreams and pollutes the sacred spaces of their imagined motherland. The "pig" analogy also symbolically violates and castrates the gendered subaltern subjects. That is why throughout the nationalist and elitist discourses in India one comes across the piggish/beastly and subhuman curse on the genitals of the gendered subaltern. Almost all the so called riots in India witness planned and well executed mutilations of the genitalia of the woman.[27] This is the context in which the poor weavers of Banaras express their fears about the vasectomy project of the district administration (161).

Iqbal the son of Mateen also becomes a weaver and he alone realizes the depth of the weaver women's doom. "He witnessed his mother's silent longing for a sari right from the time he had been a child. It was shameful! A woman, in whose house saris were woven for the entire world, could not afford even an inexpensive Banarasi sari for herself, she spent all her life in cotton dhotis [..]" (229).

The narrative concludes with the beginning of a political awakening among the weavers, the collective movement of artisans and workers for an egalitarian work culture. Iqbal carries forward the productive and creative craft of his community, though his father failed in his effort to form a co-operative society (246-47).

Though the novel breaks many stereotypes and stock images by representing the diversity and plurality of the margin, some of the analogies and motifs in the narrative are marred by exoticism and banality. The act of weaving and the weaving subject are seductively aestheticized and metaphorically eternalized in a metaphysical vein, and this takes the narrative in a wanton flight far away from material ground. The attempt to represent the peripheries of the cultural geography finds its rhythm and pace in the novelist's struggle to include himself as a live character and participant in the narrative. Though critics like Rana Singh are inclined to consider this as a continuation of the Premchand tradition of representing the peasantry and the artisan folk from closer quarters,[28] it could be better acknowledged as an attempt to trace the subaltern voice from within the margins of the cultural milieu to which Bismillah himself belongs.

Notes

1. Meenakshi Mukherjee, *Realism and Reality* (NewDelhi: Oxford UP, 1994), identifies four streams in the narrative of *Godan* from the mimetic to the dialogic, along with the binaries of the village and the city. She places the text in its troubled times and comments that it defeats any explicit notion of ideology by escaping any straightforward remedies to social problems. Also see Shashi Bhushan Upadhyay, "Representing the Underdogs: Dalits in the Literature of Premchand," *Studies in History* 18. 1 (2002): 51-80.
2. Partha Chatterjee, *The Nation and its Fragments: Colonial and Post Colonial Histories* (NewDelhi: Oxford UP, 1994). See the chapter "The Nation and its Peasants."
3. For a detailed review of the equation between Brahmanism and Hinduism, especially in the colonial/ nationalist period, see Amalendu Misra, *Identity and*

Religion: Foundations of Anti-Islamism in India (New Delhi: Sage, 2005); more particularly the chapters "Vivekanada's Hindu Regeneration Project" and "Gandhi and Political Hinduism." Misra observes that the omnipresent ideology of Brahmanism is inseparable from 'Hinduism' and even the so called secular leaders are uneasy with India's Muslim past.

4. Nobody asks why the buffalo contributing more than ninety percent of India's milk resources, is not a sacred and national animal, says Kancha Ilaiah, "Cow and Culture," *The Hindu*, 22 August 2002.

5. In his *Buffalo Nationalism* (Calcutta: Samya, 2004), Ilaiah argues that buffalo is the Indian mammal that has been giving us milk from the earliest settlement times onwards and the cow is an external beast that came to India along with the Aryans, exemplifying invasion and hegemony. See the Introduction of *Buffalo Nationalism.*

6. Govind Narain Sharma, *Premchand: Novelist and Thinker* (Delhi: Pragati, 1999) 129-35.

7. Nataraja Guru, "The Dialectics of Advaida Vedanta," *Life and Teachings of Narayana Guru, Part I: Word of the Guru* (Fernhill: East-West University, 1990), 59-73, observes: "The Advaita Vedanta [..] of Sankara was itself a revaluation of [..] Buddhist wisdom which formed its background" (60). Those who consider S Radhakrishnan as the "authentic" commentator of Sankara often repress Radhakrishnan's Hindu-Brahmanic affiliations. See for example Robert A MacDermott, introduction, *Basic Writings of S Radhakrishnan*, ed., Robert A MacDermott (Hyderabad: Orient Longman, 1980), 13-26, which says: "Radhakrishnan does not give sufficient weight to the pluralistic and dualistic strains in the Indian tradition, and his interpretation of Buddhist philosophy is notoriously inadequate" (15-16). Also see Paul Arthur Schilpp, "Fragments of a Confession," *The Philosophy of S. Radhakrishnan*, ed., Schilpp (New York: Tudor, 1952) 10-22.

8. J. Reghu, "Hindu Colonialisavum Dalitatvavum," *Mathrubhumi Weekly*, Aug 16 (2005): 26-29.

9. Uma Chakravarti, "Saffroning the Past: Of Myths, Histories and Right Wing Agendas," *Economic and Political Weekly* 33 (1998): 225-32, discusses in detail this exclusionary Hindu upper caste imagination of the past and the urge to engineer the present and future as "the rise of fascist right wing brigade." Also see her essay "Building Consent: The Middle Classes, Violence and Hindutva" in Arslan, *Communalism in India: Challenge and Response* (98-112). Gyanendra Pandey, *The Construction of Communalism in Colonial North India* (New Delhi: Oxford UP, 1990) sees the divisive politics of colonialism behind this conflict. Also see Satish Despande, "Communalising the Nation Space: Notes on the Spatial Strategies of Hindutva," *Economic and Political Weekly* 30 (1995): 3220-27. Mehdi Arslan and Janki Rajan, eds., *Communalism in India: Challenge and Response* (New Delhi: Manohar, 1994) also takes up the question of the interrelations between Nationalism and Communalism. For instance see Gyan Pandey, "Nationalism, Communalism and the Struggle over History" in the volume.
10. Rustom Bharucha, "Muslims and Others: Anecdotes, Fragments and Uncertainties of Evidence," *Economic and Political Weekly* 38 (2003): 4238-50, critiques the exclusionary mode of "othering" the minorities. For a detailed analysis of the historic alienation and separation of Muslims in India see Anwar Alam, "Democratisation of Indian Muslims," *Economic and Political Weekly* 38 (2003): 4881-85 and Asghar Ali Engineer, "Remaking Indian Muslim Identity," *Economic and Political Weekly* 26 (1991): 1036-38. Also see Sumit Sarkar and Pradeep Dutta, "Manufacturing Hatred: The Image of the Muslim in the Ramjanmabhumi Movement," in Arslan, *Communalism in India: Challenge and Response* (83-97).
11. Zoya Hasan, "More Equal But Still Not Equal: State and Inter Group Equality in Contemporary India," in Imtiaz Ahmed, *Pluralism and Equality: Values in Indian Society and Politics* (82-98).
12. P. Sainath, "Communalism and the Media," in Arslan, *Communalism in India: Challenge and Response* (136-54).

For a detailed discourse analysis of the post Gujarat Hindu hegemonic discourse in the Malayalam media see Ajay Sekher, "Monopolizing and Policing Culture: Savarna/Upper Caste Hindu Hegemonic Discourse in Malayalam Media," *New Quest* 150 (2003): 43-55.

13. See Sudhir Kakar, "Some Unconscious Aspects of Ethnic Violence in India," *Communities, Riots and Survivors in South Asia,* ed., Veena Das (New Delhi: Oxford UP, 1990) 135-43.
14. See Bharucha, specifically the section "Genocide and the Other." Also Veena Das, *Communities, Riots and Survivors in South Asia*. Also see P Sainath, "Bombay Riots of December 1992: A Report" in Arslan, *Communalism in India: Challenge and Response* (191-98).
15. M L Sondhi and Apratim Mukherjee, eds., *The Black Book of Gujarat* (New Delhi: Manas Publishers, 2002).
16. Imtiaz Ahmed, "Basic Conflict of 'We' and 'They' Between Religious Traditions, Between Hindus, Muslims and Christians in India," *Pluralism and Equality: Values in Indian Society and Politics* (New Delhi: Sage, 2000) 156-70. Also see Mushirual Hasan, "Changing position of Muslims and the political Future of Secularism in India," *Region, Religion, Caste, Gender and Culture in Contemporary India,* ed., TV Sathyamurty (NewDelhi: Oxford UP, 1996) 200-28.
17. The concept of "marginalia" is developed from Spivak and partly from Bhabha, not simply as the representation of the dispossessed from the third world but as a representation of the socio political and cultural margins that implies marginality in terms of gender, caste and class.Patriarchal and Brahmanical cultural history plays a key role in the caste and gender marginalia. Bourdieu's notions of the reproduction of inequality, symbolic violence, field, habitus and practice are also appropriated here. See Spivak, "Explanation and Culture: Marginalia," *In Other Worlds: Essays in Cultural Politics* (New York: Routledge, 1988) 103-17; Homi Bhabha, "DissemiNation: Time, Narrative and the Margins of the Modern Nation," *Nation and Narration,* ed., Homi Bhabha (London: Routledge, 1990)

291-322; and Richard Jenkins, *Pierre Bourdieu* (London: Routledge, 1992).

18. Abdul Bismillah, *Song of the Loom*, trans. Rashmi Govind (Madras: Macmillan India, 1996) 1-4.

19. Gyanendra Pandey, "The Colonial Construction of 'Communalism': British Writings on Banaras in the Nineteenth Century," in Veena Das, *Communities, Riots and Survivors in South Asia* (94-134). The Sangh Parivar demolished the sets of Dipa Mehta's film *Water* in early 2004 here. The film was about the Hindu widows of 1930s. Mehta had to complete the film in Srilanka later following Government restrictions in India.

20. All subsequent quotations are from Abdul Bismillah, *Song of the Loom*, trans. Rashmi Govind (Madras: Macmillan India, 1996).

21. For a discussion of questions concerning the cultural plurality and social complexity of Indian Muslim communities see Mushirul Hasan, "'Majorities' and 'Minorities' in Modern South Asian Islam: A Historian's Perspective," *Caste and Social Stratification Among Muslims,* ed., Imtiaz Ahmed (New Delhi: Oxford UP, 1978) 141-55; Sayyed Zainuddin, "Islam, Social Stratification and Empowerment of Muslim OBCs," *Economic and Political Weekly* 38 (2003): 4898-99; Seik Rahim Mondel, "Social Structure, OBCs and Muslims," *Economic and Political Weekly* 38 (2003): 4892-97; Irfan Ahmed, "A Different Jihad: Dalit Muslims' Challenge to Ashraf Hegemony," *Economic and Political Weekly* 38 (2003): 4886-91; and Pervaiz Nazir, "Social Structure, Ideology and Language: Caste Among Muslims," *Economic and Political Weekly* 28 (1993): 2897-99.

22. Both subaltern and gendered subaltern or the new subaltern are conceptual categories extended from Spivak. See Spivak, "On the New Subaltern," *Subaltern Studies XI: Community, Gender, Violence,* ed., Partha Chatterjee and Pradip Jaganathan (New Delhi: Permanent Black, 2000) 305-34. And also "Can the Subaltern Speak?" *Marxism and the Interpretation of Culture*, ed., Carey Nelson and Lawrence Grossberg (Urbana: U of Indiana P, 1988) 51-88.

23. See Prem Chowdhary, "Enforcing Cultural Codes: Gender and Violence in Northern India," *Economic and Political Weekly* 32 (1997): 1019-28; Vrinda Nabar, *Caste as Woman* (New Delhi: Penguin, 1995); and Seemanthini Niranjana, *Gender and Space: Femininity, Sexualization and the Female Body* (New Delhi: Sage, 2001).

24. Ranjit Sau, "Recognition to Witchcraft: Illegal and Ill-founded," *Economic and Political Weekly* 38 (2003): 5325-26; Meera Nanda, *Prophets Facing Backward: Postmodern Critiques of Science and Hindu Nationalism* (New Delhi: Permanent Black, 2004).

25. Kancha Ilaiah, "Beef, BJP and Food Rights of People," *Economic and Political Weekly* 31 (1996): 1444-45; and "Cow and Culture," *The Hindu*, 21 July 2002.

26. B R Ambedkar, *Buddha and His Dhamma* (Bombay: SCP, 1957) and also Gail Omvedt, *Budhism in India: Challenging Brahmanism and Caste* (New Delhi: Sage, 2003).

27. Report of the Joint Delegation of Women's Organizations, "Women and Communal Riots," Arslan, *Communalism in India: Challenge and Response* (150-54).

28. Rana Singh, "Weaver's World: The Threadbare Shawl of Abdul Bismillah," *Where Cultural Symbols Meet: Images of Varanasi* (Varanasi: Tara, 1989) 24-45.

2

Brahmanic Patriarchy: *Rudali*, *Woodworm*

> It is the women who are ruined by the Malik Mahajans who turn into whores. Nonsense they are a separate caste. (*Rudali* 80)

> God! I am fortunate to have the purest air and the brightest blood in my body. I have not knelt in prayer for any woman. My mind dear sir is the body of a swan. All these years I have made use of women in a wonderful manner. I didn't get trapped in a knot at the end of a sari. I am untainted and chaste. (*Woodworm* 10)

Mahasweta Devi's fiction has been widely read and critically theorized as a powerful representational attempt from the point of view of the third world marginalia.[1] Questions of caste/gender/class are raised and rethought in the textual and contextual premises of her radical and interventionist narrative praxis. The plight of the muted and the silenced, the cause of the gendered subaltern, women's empowerment and radical feminist realism – these are some of the positions attributed to her fiction.[2] In *Rudali* Devi portrays the low caste woman both as victim and as a potentially subversive agent in the phallogocentric order of Brahmanical patriarchy.[3]

The de-sentimentalized and detached narrative presents the hopeless predicament of Sanichari and other low caste women in a North Indian village ruled by Brahmanic patriarchy in the latter half of the twentieth century.[4] The nexus of caste, phallocentrism and feudalism in this village breaks the stereotypes of nationalist conceptions like Gandhian Gram Swaraj.[5] The occidental autocracy of the village communities was the self-rule of caste, which in Dr Ambedkar's words was the "ditch of regionalism and the den of ignorance and parochialism."[6] The Tahad village is a typical representation of such a community:

> In Tahad village, ganjus and dushads were in majority. Sanichari was a ganju by caste. Like other villagers her life too was lived in desperate poverty. Her mother-in-law used to say it was because Sanichari was born on inauspicious Saturday that her destiny was full of suffering [..] to herself she would say – huh! Because I was born on and named after a Saturday that made me an unlucky daughter-in-law! You were born on a Monday – was your life any happier? Somri, Budha, Moongri, Bishri – do any of them have happier lives? (54)

So caste and gender affiliations were the decisive elements of social /human status and identity and were the material reality of the Indian village. As a sample and iconic metonymy of the larger national body, the narrative here explicates this village reality of Brahmanic patriarchy, which at the same time is also the national Indian reality. The socio cultural constructs of caste and gender are thus problematized from the very beginning of the novel. The emphasis here is on the gender innuendo of caste patriarchy.[7] Sanichari, a Ganju woman, is a representative of the gendered subaltern, the subject who is both low caste and woman at the same time.

The gendered subaltern's condition of unimaginable material misery and oppression could only be historicized through representative subjects.[8] See the descriptions of the torturous and hellish death of a low caste woman and the hardship of the living dead:

> Her mother-in-law died in great pain, of dropsy, lying in her own excrement, crying out, over and over, 'food, give me food!' It was pouring that night. Sanichari and her sister-in-law lowered the old woman on to the ground. If the rites weren't carried out before the night

> was over they would have to bear the cost of the repentance rites for keeping the corpse in the house overnight. And there wasn't even a cupful of grain in the house! So Sanichari was forced to go from neighbour to neighbour in the pouring rain. Dragging the neighbours home with her, and handling all the arrangements for the cremation, she was so busy that there was no time to cry. So what if there wasn't? the old woman had given her so much trouble that even if Sanichari had tried to cry she wouldn't have been able to wring out many tears. (55)

The misery and the historic experience of injustice dehumanize the subjects to a state of insensitivity. That is why Sanichari, like the vast majority of women in India is presented as un-emotional, bereft of her intimate emotions, and even of tears. Sanichari is aware that it is the daily struggles under oppression and the everyday realities of injustice and double standards that degrade and dehumanize women:

> Their grief must have hardened into stone within them. To herself Sanichari had sighed with relief. Is it possible to feed so many mouths on the meager scrapings they bring home after labouring on the malik's field? Two dead, just as well. At least their own stomachs would be full. (55)

The narrative adds the dimension of class here.[9] But clearly it is in tandem with the larger social and cultural determinants of caste and gender that the class issue is narrativized. And again it should be read in the context of the caste feudalism of the Indian village. The Maliks, Mahajans and Maharajas of the hamlets are caste lords and are anointed as such by Brahmanic patriarchy. It is thus true that these narrative contexts turn women as the real victims of the forces of caste/class/gender. There have been attempts to reduce this dialogic discourse into one that is driven by economic determinism; such attempts too are neutralized in the reading.[10]

Descriptions of caste oppression and material violence are present throughout the narrative. The serene and idyllic village landscape is littered with caste curses and other instances of symbolic and metaphoric violence. According to the Vaid (physician) of the village, "the lower castes have no patience, no ability to bear up" (61). Note that the curse is always on the caste and on one's ancestors and the lineage rather than on individual errors and shortcomings.

Such barbarous treatment from the social superiors and feudal lords along with class oppression and material economic misery become endless, especially for the gendered subaltern at the bottom of the hierarchy: "the lice medicine killed the creatures in Sanichari's hair. After sleeping comfortably she realized that her sleepless nights had been caused by the lice, not mental anguish. No matter how grief stricken one is, a work worn body is bound to sleep well" (67). Thus the individual as well as the social body are in decay and rot and need a reformist intervention badly.

Even the death of the feudal lord is the occasion for establishing caste honour and supremacy. The upper castes lament not for the dead, but in fear of losing caste distinctions and privileges: "Hai, Chacha! As long as you were alive, the lower castes never dared raise their heads. For fear of you the sons of dushads and ganjus never dared attend government schools! Now who will take care of all these things?" (68). Their fundamental concern is with keeping the Bahujans away from schools, and the dead man was of use in it and that is why his death is being mourned. The barbaric core of the Hindu caste village is explicated here through these Rajput clans and their caste-centred world view. They themselves were mere footmen in the army of the king and later acquired social and political power through militarization. Later in the narrative this Neo Kshatriya formation of the Shudra footmen is briefly described. As seen elsewhere in the country, once they achieve this Neo Brahmanic stature they become the ardent and devoted protectors of the Brahmanic order and its caste ethos. Even the burial of the dead becomes a ceremonial occasion for the exhibition of the caste affiliation of the dead person in such a context: "We must perform the ceremonies and burial with pomp and splendour. Dress up the body, place him on a big bed and inform our entire Rajput clan" (68).

The caste patriarchy's ultimate perversion could be identified in the forced custom of making the low caste women weep over the body of the dead upper caste male. This humiliating and symbolically mutilating assault over the material and emotional domains of the gendered subaltern could be contextualized and read as the historically fetishistic, genocidal and perverted core of Brahmanic patriarchy. The title *Rudali* refers to the humiliating task of the low caste women who are made to wail over their caste master's death. This forced misery is called the "Rudali work."

> They (upper castes) need rudalis to wail over the corpse. They have got hold of two whores. In the household of the masters, whores weep for the dead. These two were Bhairab Singh's whores at one time. Now they are wizened crows. They will be no good. The two of you go, wail, cry, accompany the corpse. You will get money, rice. On the day of the kriya ceremony you will get clothes and food. (70)

Though she was totally against it at the beginning, Sanichari also becomes a Rudali because of material constraints. It is the caste lords who create whores and wailers out of the low caste women. Both the body and the mind of the gendered subaltern is the property of the caste lord who has the sovereign power over the subaltern bodies/ minds/spirits. The Rajput Maliks literally forced the tag of "whores" on to the low caste women and constructed a descent of prostitute wailers, and the caste called Rudalis.

> Singhs of this world treat their labourers and whores alike - they tread them into the mud [..] what vicious bastards that lot are! The worst is Gambhir Singh. He

> kept a whore, had a daughter by her. As long as the whore was alive, he kept the child in comfort. When the mother died, he told the girl, a whore's daughter is a whore - practise your profession and support yourself [..] the girl is now rotting in Tohri, in the randi bazaar. From a five-rupee whore she's down to a five-paisa whore. (70-1)

The Rajput legacy of assuming Kshatriya status and Brahmanical legitimacy is also circulated among the villagers as subaltern folk tales and secret lore:

> The tale Dulan told them was very significant. It explained how the ruthless Rajputs infiltrated this remote area of tribals, and from zamindars gradually built themselves up to the status of jotedars/ moneylenders and established themselves as the masters of the area. The Rajputs were the warriors in the army of the Raja of Chottanagpur. About two hundred years ago in protest against the cruelties practiced against them the Kol tribals revolted. The Raja immediately sent out the army to put down the uprising. Even after the rebellion was suppressed the warriors' aggression was not sated. They went on a rampage killing innocent tribals and burning down villages. So Harda and Donka Munda started sharpening their arrows and a fresh tribal uprising was imminent. Then the Raja sent his sardars to the sparsely populated Tahad region. He told them take as much land as is covered by throwing your swords in the air...that's how they come to be the masters of this region. (73)

Thus the whole history of invasion and aggression is narrativized at different levels with inter-textual references within the text. This again is typical of Mahasweta's fiction that falls back upon historical and even social anthropological research and archival data. *Breast Stories* is another example in which the gendered subaltern Dopdi is such a fictional representation of a community of others and outcastes marginalized along caste and gender lines.[11]

Sanichari in *Rudali* too is an individual representation of such a community that is always outside the texts of culture and history. Almost all of Mahasweta Devi's female protagonists articulate the larger questions of the community of people who are erased from the discourses of mainstream fiction. The deliberately detached and de-sentimentalized voice dominating the narrative could perhaps be contextualized on this premise. The texts break apart the stereotypes of intimacy, romantic nostalgia and evocative sensuality associated with an appealing narration in order to emphasize the mundane and material inequality implied by caste and gender.

The Brahmanic Hindu system survives on the labour potential of the Bahujans and on the bio power of the gendered subaltern.[12] The company of "whores" is literally produced and maintained for the purposes of hegemony. Thus the wailing whores are not only made but are kept, preserved and rated too according to the commodity price index. "Lachman Singh has ordered that ten, twenty, and whatever it takes he wants good rudalis. Two hundred rupees have been budgeted for this" (71). Their wailing potential is nurtured and promoted with adequate resources. "And feed them well – they can't mourn convincingly on an empty stomach" (71).

But the problematic emerges as the narrative fuses class outlook with a caste/gender perspective to focus on the ideological underpinnings of caste patriarchy:

> Business prospered. There was such a demand for the pair who wailed at Bhairab Singh's funeral, that it was almost like a war of prestige. Soon not just the landlords and moneylenders but lalas and sahus began to ask for Sanichari. In fact, when Gokul lala's father died he said, come everyday till the kriya ceremony, Sanichari. (75)

On certain occasions class seems to overtake caste as forces of caste defilement are suppressed by concerns about class status: "His(lord's) mother is left to lie in her own excrement all day. Once every evening Moti the dushad woman cleans her up – no one is concerned about loss of caste or defilement any longer, it seems" (77).

The absurdity of this class angle is that it is the low castes who are at the bottom of things even in the class analytical framework; and they are unable to climb up economically on a vertical axis from within this "class system." This pretentious and ideologically strategic class mode of narration is self-exposed and cancelled by the dialogic narrative discourse itself on occasions:

> When someone died in a malik mahajan household, the amount of money spent on the death ceremonies immediately raised the prestige of the family. The status of the rudalis also rose. The price for this was paid by the dushads, dhobis, ganjus and kols, from the hides of whom the overlords extracted the sums they had overspent. (80)

Such is the degrading conditions in which the low caste woman is destined to live: "It is the women who are ruined by the Malik Mahajans who turn into whores. Nonsense they are a separate caste" (80). But Sanichari rises to the occasion and seizes the opportunity by making it an act of revenge and expression of historical dissent. "Sanichari thought that perhaps her tears had been reserved for the time when she would have to feed herself by selling them" (72). Whenever she gets an opportunity she strikes at the heart of caste patriarchy: "Sanichari puts on an innocent air and asks – But I heard that the upper castes never got smallpox? That it was a disease of the poor and lower castes? That's why we take the government vaccination as well as appease the gods" (78). This kind of a feeble and postponed protest or defensive empowerment could be identified in the central character as the narrative advances.

The gendered subaltern occasionally uses the frameworks and hidden structures of caste patriarchy to derail its own operations from within, though this is done hesitantly. The position of the historical victim and her struggle for self-defense and survival are articulated somewhat ambiguously by the text. That is why even in the concluding scene the rising protest wail of the Rudalis before the master's corpse becomes an apology for a rebellion and an articulation from within a mediated and confined space already marked and permitted by the Brahmanic patriarchy and never breaks and subverts the system (91).

The detached narrative voice that attempts a de-sentimentalized representation of woman as whore also problematizes the "whore" discourse popularized by patriarchy . Patriarchy stereotypes and labels any subaltern woman as a "whore" but the repeated use of the word throughout the narrative also draws attention to the ideology of this mode of marking and addressing the woman ("You are the daughter of a whore" and "a whole crowd of whores" (81)). In that sense the social effect of the narrative discourse is that of reiteration of the status quo and of maintaining the balanced power relations existing in society.

Such consensual generalizations and compromises with the existing order and the class analytical modes of orthodox Marxist analyses could also be identified as the cause of the strange mix-up of the class factor in certain weak points in the narrative that defeats itself in the overarching effect of caste and gender cultural contexts. The caste core of the context rushes back with a vengeance as the class mode tries to take over. That is why even after assuming an occupational class status, the Rudalis transform themselves into a caste, that too a gendered caste, specifically a low caste of "whores." This could again be identified as the central tension or contradiction in the social practice of Mahasweta's fiction and her narrative praxis. Most of her texts try to tackle and address the tension in caste/class/ gender relations in the historic context/s of the Brahmanic caste patriarchy in North and Eastern India and when they fail and cancel their own discourses of counter-hegemonic and subversive politics, they do so in response to the class burden of the middle/upper caste Indian literati. The class hangover of the intervening middle class/caste activist is therefore under question and scrutiny as a reluctance to address the issue of caste and its historical exclusions, its unimaginable barbarism revealed in the very act of its avoidance/suppression in the present. The ambivalence of the activist writer and the ethical dilemmas of the intervention narrativized in the fictional text are problematized in such a reading and the question of agency and voice for the subaltern is foregrounded. This once again throws up the fundamental cultural materialist questions of caste and gender in the historic premises and discursive contexts of the Brahmanic caste patriarchy. It also brings to light fiction's affiliations with the dominant and hegemonic ideologies and affects and its limitations in radical praxis. This is also the background against which the politics of disguise and avoidance in the novel *Woodworm* invites critical attention.

When Sirshendu Mukhopadhyay's *Woodworm* was first published in 1967 in Bengali it was widely read and acknowledged as an existential narrative that depicted the identity crisis and alienation of the protagonist Shyam in an increasingly urban, middle class Calcutta. Critics and commentators were quick to identify the strong and lasting imprint of Kafka's *The Metamorphosis* and Camus' *The Outsider* in it.[13] But when we place the text in its cultural context the story that emerges is much more complex and conflit-ridden.

Shyam Chakrabarty, son of Kamalaksha Chakrabarty, born and brought up in an upper middle class Bengali Brahman family is the protagonist of the novel. He is the deputy chief of a corporate house called Saint and Miller. But he quits his job because his boss calls him "bastard." He experiences a deep psycho-social crisis that leads him to a life of murder, adultery and endless moral turmoil. The striking elements of his behavior are violence and sexual perversion. His moral corruption is indicated by the way he kills a motorbike rider in the street by reflecting light on to his eyes. He plays with women in an endless abusive game that explains the depth of his psycho-sexual ruin and the split in his psychic personality. As the narrative closes we see him plunge deeper and deeper into an ego-centric game that is an expression of his withdrawal into himself. This withdrawal, needless to say, assumes new meanings in the context of the critique of the sovereign self related to Brahmanic masculinity made in Chapter I.

An egocentric or oedipal psyche that tries to master and manipulate fellow beings could easily be identified in this psycho-sexual drama. The fascist oedipal subject of the novel kills and subordinates upwardly mobile men and charming women. He controls their life energy, mobility and sexuality. This centered subjectivity craves for total and comprehensive control and agency. At the heart of its seductive core lies the desire for governmentality. Its craving and yearning is for absolute power and totalizing hegemony. This omnipotent and all pervasive hegemonic agency wants to intervene in everything and wants to represent everyone. The subjectivity that represents all and intervenes everywhere like this can be called a fascist subjectivity. It never compromises in matters of control, power, autonomy and governmentality. Actually it evades the slightest challenge to its regime and retreats into the darkness of the underworld like a blood-sucking vampire, as is narrated at the end of the novel. It eludes and escapes all egalitarian resolutions and de-centering democratic formations. Violence, hierarchy, subordination and exploitation are its classic paradigms and potential sources. This fascist subject is nothing but a representative of the hegemonic subject position, which in Indian cultural and historical context could be termed as that of Brahmanic patriarchy.

The crisis and alienation that the subject experiences, following a slight threat to his totalitarian existence (the boss calling him bastard) could be regarded as an iconic threat to the hegemony and totalizing power of representation (in the post-independent constitutional context the power elite had to share political power with the people). He collapses in the face of increasing challenges (people's collective movements and attacks on power monopolies) to his hegemony. But even in ruins he could not change and continues his parasitism (the vampirism of surviving on the lifeblood and toil of the people) and hides away his countenance in earth as the narrative closes. Thus this bloodsucking and seductive vampire is nothing but a classic metaphor of the hegemonic subject that assumes fierce proportions with inputs from patriarchy and elitist cultural discourses. In analogous situations in the Western context of capitalism, Deleuze and Guattari would call it an "oedipal subject" that tries to master and manipulate everything around it. They have very precisely identified the fascist underpinnings and implications of such a subject.[14] In his preface to *Anti Oedipus*, Foucault identifies the centrality of desire as it is expressed and repressed in specific cultural contexts and connects it to political fascism as well as to the fascism within us that desires domination of the other and the self.

The cause for Chakrabarty's quitting the job too is unusual and suspicious: "is drawing, his superior Hari Majumbdar had said 'bastard' in an aside. Majumdar used obscenities with every breath. Besides, all these days Shyam was emulating Hari Majumdar in his behavior and manner of speech." (1)

So it is implied that it is a matter concerning a 'Chakrabarty' and a 'Majumdar.' It is a question of surnames and its legacies, a clash of ancient significations and titles, that of Brahmanic caste epithets and of caste hierarchy itself. That is why he "soon realized that a single abusive word had actually released a ghost in his brain" (2).

At this moment it would be significant to remember that the modernist writing in Indian languages often evaded or under-represented key socio cultural questions like that of caste and patriarchy. It was more interested in representing alienation, angst and other borrowed fads. The political question of caste/gender as well as questions pertaining to the hegemonic subject formations are explored in detail in the present rereading. The psychological crisis and schizophrenic drama that unfold in the narrative would acquire a new resonance in such a reading.

First, let us look at the patriarchal psyche of the male protagonist. Soon after he resigns his job Chakrabarty indulges in a sort of woman hunt, going after one woman after another. He is a typical womanizer. He craves to control and manipulate the female subjects; he wants to master their bodies and minds. What he demands is total submission and perpetual subordination and not sex and bodily union. Thus macho perversion and fascist desire for comprehensive control could be identified in his actions and inactions with a range of women from Brinda, Madhabi, and Leela to Itu. While Leela has a Brahmanic surname Bhattacharya, Itu has nothing. Itu is a commonplace Bengali name denoting easy availability and access and it is no wonder Chakarbarty uses her as a mere sex slave, a cheap sex toy. He literally plays with her body and spirit: "The game was growing on him. He said cheerfully, 'play, Itu. Come on, play. You are even more beautiful now'" (22).

On the other hand, he is very cautious and concerned in relation to the Bhattacharya girl. She is everything elevated and refined for him. She is the centre of good taste and refined desire for Chakrabarty (whose surname literally means the emperor). This hierarchized notion of gender and the casteist attitude to sexuality are the chief tenets of Brahmanic patriarchy that not only governs the sexuality of Brahman women in the clan but also expands sexual colonies outside it even among Shudra women. See how Chakrabarty tortures his gendered subjects in classic fascist fashion, reminding us of the nightmares like the ones in Pasolini's *Salo*:

> Hey…Itu, not there…don't fall down. You'll spoil the game. Don't give up so fast. Don't stop. If you stop I will boo you. If you stop you are an old crow. If you stop you are a lump of clay. Go round and round Itu…till you turn into a *shadow*…let me come to you with my *desire*. (28)

So non-Brahmanical women are mere babbles in his hand, wanton flies which he kills for his sport. The fascist taskmaster enslaves, tortures and eliminates "inferior" women of other races with his omnipotent male desire that consumes everything and targets all. Now see how he handles the male subjects like Minu.

Like Itu, Minu, another common Benglai without a surname, haunts Shyam. Minu is the haunting male figure in his dreams. Minu tortures him and he is presented as a brute force, a representation of the unlimited, uncouth male force that threatens Shyam's hegemonic aspirations. This image of the violent subversive dark male force that comes from the depth of the underworld or the unconscious recurs in the text as well in the split psyche of the hero and could be placed as the subversive threat that comes from the margins of the social order. An inevitable threat and challenge without a Brahmanic surname from the Bahujan premises.

The challenge that Chakrabarty experiences in his confrontation with the motorbike rider is similar to this. It is a mobile threat from the new "other" world; it destabilizes the hierarchical power equilibrium and displaces the socio political status quo. It is a driving force from the lower strata and is an icon of zooming mobility, which is upwardly and forwardly targeted. The oedipal subject could not stand it and it subverts it at the very first glance. Shyam Chakrabarty as a total zyborg of high-tech Brahmanism has no hesitation whatsoever to exterminate the 'other' man in cold blood. Towards the end of the narrative it is revealed that the victim who dies in a hospital was a poor man with familial responsibilities: "He had remained unconscious till death. He was married two years ago and had a baby daughter" (100). The picture is complete when we connect it to the casual thought of the killer after the incident, yes it is that ancient grudge against mobility that wants to reassert hierarchy and hegemony forever: "He just couldn't remember the reason why he had an ancient grudge against all motorbike riders" (39).

Chakrabarty is always keen to assert his hierarchical and sexual/gender superiority in relation to people in general and women in particular. He is almost beastly in his desiring gaze: "You are getting worse every day Shyam [..] you have learnt to stare at me like a wolf" (9) says Madhabi. He always imagines himself as the ultimate sexual being, a fatal male centre of desire and refined charms. His own rhetoric goes thus: "in my body resided the purest air and the brightest blood. I have never done any bowing and scraping for woman" (9). So in his ego centric imagination women are always falling for him and he holds the most superior, coveted phallus. This again brings in the analogy of the phallogocentric discourse of Brahmanic patriarchy.

See how he connects this discourse to the formulations suggesting divine and patriarchal rights. For him masculinity is a godly lineage, a patrilineal possession, linked to a discourse that sounds exactly like "the twice born metaphysics" of Brahmanism narrativized in *Samskara* (see the next chapter).

> 'God! I am fortunate to have the purest air and the brightest blood in my body. I have not knelt in prayer for any woman. My mind dear sir is the body of a swan. All these years I have made use of women in a wonderful manner. I didn't get trapped in a knot at the end of a sari. I am untainted and chaste.' (10)

Note the racial supremacist discourse in operation along with the sexist and anti-woman rhetoric. The fascist, hegemonic and oedipal character of Chakrabarty is inscribed and exposed in many of his utterances through out the text. The oedipal core of his subjectivity is exposed in his queer love-hate relationship to Minu. Minu is a threat and an enchantment for Shyam at the same time. He tortures and enthralls him at the same time in his dreamy memories:

> Shyam wished he could go and face Minu now. Slap him on the back and say, 'how's everything buddy!' Then lower his voice and say, 'take me in your gang mate? These two hands can mange a machine gun or a knuckle-duster; plunge a knife into a stomach as if it is butter [..].' He wanted to be on equal terms with Minu, sit face to face and speak in an intimate voice. (22)

Another important feature of his mental make up is his deep devotion and passion for Brahmanic texts like the *Gita*. In the context of his hegemonic subjectivity it is not strange that a corporate executive, a booming business magnate like him knows the *Gita* by heart! He is also addicted to the hegemonic hermeneutics of Brahmanic metaphysics contained in such works as *Raja Yoga* and *Life Divine*:

> *Raja Yoga* and *Life Divine* were my daily reading. I know the *Bhagavat Gita* by heart [...] I had gone quite far on the path of asceticism [..] whenever I sat in meditation my skin crawled, my body felt light as air, I would even see an occasional glow of light [..] stood with my hand across my chest like Vivekananda [..] in those days when I was twenty-one. (42-3)

The ideological underpinnings of the hegemonic subject is indicated here. It is nothing but the cultural and religious nationalist ideology of Hindu revivalism exemplified in the Vedic and Vedantic hermeneutics of Vivekananda and Aurobindo. Recent scholarship has identified them as the proto texts of cultural nationalism and religious fundamentalism that emerged in the wake of anti-colonial Hindu Brahmanic nationalism and the Bengal renaissance.[15] Also note his intense affiliation to the *Gita* (he knows it by heart!) which is the iconic Brahmanic text that preserved Chathurvarnya and the caste system and ensured Brahmanic hegemony for millennia.

Chakrabarty is always keen to establish and signify his Hindu Brahmanic identity as distinct from that of his Muslim fellow beings. Even in a city tram he remembers it: "Suddenly Shyam remembered that Irfan was a Muslim, that he himself was a Hindu…It seemed incredible that he was the son of Kamalaksha Chakrabarty" (66). Even in his perverted and weird encounters with "girls" he repeatedly invokes and sustains his Hindu Brahmanic patriarchal legacy. Before Leela he is all the more charged up: "My name is Shyam Chakrabarty. My father was Kamalaksha Chakrabarty. We belong to the Shandilya group of families. My ancestral home is in Banikhara" (91).

Thus a sense of hierarchical distinction, racial/caste and gender superiority in relation to women and Bahujans, perpetrated with the support of the obscurantist metaphysics of Brahmanism is narrativized through this complex character. The woodworm that permeates and consumes the whole structure from within is therefore a just metaphor for the oedipal, fascist and hegemonic subjectivity of Brahmanic patriarchy. Naturally its victims are Bahujans and women, struggling to break away from the shackles of Brahmanic patriarchy. A democratic and egalitarian de-centering is impossible since even in the closing lines of the narrative this oedipal subject retreats back to its under ground, it digs its head into the earth (106) in perpetual avoidance, escaping the material reality and its ethical demands, leaving no scope for socialization.

Notes

1. Gayatri Spivak, introduction, *Breast Stories,* by Mahasweta Devi (Calcutta: Seagull, 1992) 1-12. Also see "A Literary Representation of the Subaltern: A Woman's Text from the Third world," *In Other Worlds: Essays in Cultural Politics* (NewYork: Routledge, 1988) 241-66. And

"Can the Subaltern Speak?," *Marxism and the Interpretation of Culture*, ed. Cary Nelson and Laurence Grossberg (Urbana: U of Illinois P, 1988) 51-88.

2. Tony Beck and Tirthankar Bose, "Dispossession, Degradation and Empowerment of Peasantry and the Poor in Benglai Fiction," *Economic and Political Weekly* 30 (1995): 441-48. The paper argues that in the 70s itself Devi achieved a new construction of the poor in Bengali fiction and her view of society is subaltern and prompts change as she relocates power and redefines human worth.
3. Uma Chakravarty, "Conceptualizing Brahmanical Patriarchy in Early India: Gender, Caste, Class and State," *Economic and Political Weekly* 28 (1993): 579-85 describes the Brahmanic Hindu world in which an extreme form of social stratification is practiced by which women and low castes are subjected to humiliating conditions of existence. Caste hierarchy and gender hierarchy are the organizing principles of this social order. In this even upper caste women are enslaved to maintain not only patrilineal succession but also caste purity. For the details of this caste - gender nexus see Vasantha and Kalpana Kannabiran, "Caste and Gender: Understanding the Dynamics of Power and Violence," *Economic and Political Weekly* 26 (1991): 2130-33.
4. For historical, socio political and cultural details see K L Sharma, ed., *Social Inequality in India: Profiles of Caste, Class and Social Mobility* (New Delhi: Rawat, 2001), especially the essay by Andre Beteille, "The Reproduction of Inequality: Occupation, Caste and Family." Also see Sekhar Bandopadhyay, *Caste, Culture and Hegemony: Social Domination in Colonial Bengal* (New Delhi: Sage, 2004) for the same question with specific reference to Bengal.
5. Prem Chowdhary, "Enforcing Cultural Codes: Gender and Violence in Northern India," *Economic and Political Weekly* 32 (1997): 1019-28 analyses how caste controls gender identity and female sexuality in North Indian villages.
6. B R Ambedkar, *Complete Works,* vol.2 (Bombay: Govt. of Maharashtra, 1986) 34.

7. Vrinda Nabar, *Caste as Woman* (New Delhi: Penguin, 1995) illustrates the cultural implications of being a woman in the Indian context of Brahmanic patriarchy.
8. Seemanthini Niranjana, *Gender and Space: Femininity, Sexualization and the Female Body* (New Delhi: Sage, 2001) explores the gendering of the social and bodily spaces and sites that serve the purposes of patriarchal hegemony.
9. For a critique of class analysis from a cultural perspective in the west see John Guillory, "Literary Critic as Intellectual: Class Analysis and the Crisis of the Humanities," *Rethinking Class: Literary Studies and Social Formations*, eds., Dimock and Gilmore (Columbia: Columbia UP, 1994) 145-49.
10. See for example Anjum Katyal, "The Metamorphosis of Rudali" in Mahasweta Devi, *Rudali* (Calcutta: Seagull, 1997) 1-53. The chunk of the argument is that the individual is historicized to explicate the context and a subaltern view of economy, polity and society. Suggestions on the sidelining of gender by the class discourse too could be traced here.
11. Mahasweta Devi, *Breast Stories,* trans. Gayatri Spivak (Calcutta: Seagull, 1992).
12. Tanika Sarkar, "Reflections on Birati Rape Cases: Gender Ideology in Bengal," *Economic and Political Weekly* 26 (1991): 215-18 historicizes this patriarchal hegemony over the sexualities of subaltern woman and observes that the socialist critique of bourgeois decadence excluded modern patriarchy and caste hierarchy. Biswamoy Pati, "Women, Rape and the Left," *Economic and Political Weekly* 26 (1991): 219-20 also comments on the Left's historical avoidance/silence of patriarchy in Bengal and the role of the press in abetting it.
13. Nabaneeta Dev Sen, introduction, *Woodworm,* by Sirshendu Mukhopadhyay, trans. Shampa Banerjee (Madras: Macmillan India, 1996) 1-12.
14. Gilles Deleuze and Felix Guattari, *Anti Oedipus: Capitalism and Schizophrenia* (London: Athlone, 1983) 34-36.
15. Jyotirmaya Sharma, *Hindutva: Exploring the Idea of Hindu Nationalism* (New Delhi: Viking and Penguin, 2003). Also see Amalendu Misra, *Identity and Religion: Foundations of Anti-Islamism in India* (New Delhi: Sage, 2005), specifically chapters "Vivekananda's Regenerated Hinduism" and "Gandhi and Political Hinduism."

3

Revisiting the Village : *Samskara, Gramayana*

> It is neither Brahman nor Shudra, a carcass, a stinking carcass. [..] A snake is also a twice born, if you happen to see a dead snake you have to perform the proper rites for it.
>
> (*Samskara* 7, 19)
>
> O master we are mere pebbles in your hands [...] Until my death I will work in the field and serve my master.
>
> (*Gramayana* 174, 452)

The worldview of Anantha Murthy's *Samskara* as expressed in the first epigraph is confined in socio cultural binaries. *Samskara*'s world is characterized by its hierarchical structure that stretches from the Brahman head to the Shudra limbs following the Varna Dharma analogy of Brahmanic Hinduism.[1] With the lowest Savarna category of Shudra ends its worldview that annihilates the very existence of the real majority of people, the Dalit Bahujans, on whose labour and surplus the whole "Vedic" system survives. The "Antyajas" or "Chandals" are literally absent in this map of Brahmanism's cultural nationalist geography.[2] Even the translator A K Ramajunan in his notes elaborates/limits the scope of the low caste as Shudra.[3] The space of Bahujans is still outside the Brahmanic/ Savarna nation as well as the village, even in fictional narration done in the late sixties, almost two decades after the formation of a democratic republic.[4] Such fictional narrations could point towards many things in the post republican socio political context. The second coming of Brahmanism's absolute hegemony, its writing, its gaze, its epistemology and its neo nationalist world order are only some of them.

While summarizing and commenting on the critical responses to *Samskara*, Meenakshi Mukherjee also de-contextualizes the narrative from its undeniable discursive contexts of Brahmanism and patriarchy and universalizes it as an allegory of a "casteless wanderer." According to her "the question need not be connected to Hinduism, it is a universal problem of a man who has equated himself with a particular role" and to read it the other way is "to limit it."[5] As a scholar who worked on this in the mid eighties with out the backup of much feminist and subaltern theoretical insights she also contributes to the universalistic appeal of the narrative. In its "cosmic and liberal" discourse even reptiles are given the status of the "twice born" (see the second part of the first epigraph), but the basic communities of human beings are not even given the human status, instead they are condemned eternally as the "Chandals" and the "Pariah." The text reflects this ideology through the voice of Shankaraya, the priest of Parijatapura:

> According to Brahmin thinking, 'a snake is also a twice born,' if you happen to see a dead snake you have to perform the proper rites for it. You shouldn't eat till you have done so. (19)

Two simple questions arise here, apart from the ideology's explicit political implications pertaining to the denial of the very human existence of the Bahujans. These are firstly, whether outcastes will be allowed to do the last rites (which is forbidden in their own death) for this snake, and secondly, from where does the food come afterwards, that is who actually produces the food grain, tilling in the field and working in the mud? Perhaps Brahmanism could take the help of the double-speak metaphysics of its ancient "Vedic and Vedantic" texts here, of the texts that legitimized naked barbarism and hegemony. But before we go in to the details of the text it is also interesting to read the sub-text to this particular episode, the notes provided by the translator that form an apology of sort for such hegemonic discourses from the contemporary world:

> Twice born; Dvija, the epithet applies not only to brahmins and the other two upper castes (kshtriya 'warrior', vaisya 'tradesman') but also to birds, snakes, various grains, and tooth etc.- anything that may be said to have two births(e.g. birds and snakes are born as eggs and reborn from them). Snakes are considered sacred and therefore should be cremated ceremoniously. (151)

The divine-right metaphysics and the religious obscurantism of the elite classes that acquires legitimacy through writing and publication are quite evident here. The Bahujans could have a sigh of partial relief that the twice born status is also denied to the Shudras, their immediate lords and torturers, who mediate between the top and bottom (with regional variations, for instance Mahatma Phule was a Shudra) for the "Sanatana" sustenance of this most perverted power structure in human history![6] One of the fundamental tenets of the Brahmanic hegemonic discourse in India has been its metaphysics of the second birth. Dvija, the twice born, a synonym for the Brahman thus achieved ideological and strategic epistemological canonization in the post-Buddhist period through the pan-Indian metanarratives of Sanskrit through centuries of internal imperialism that could be termed as Sanskritization or Hinduization.[7] It is this obscurantist and parasitic ideology of Brahmanism that is reflected in the text of *Samskara*. By repressing the signification of the natural human birth from the womb and genitals of the mother/ woman, Brahmanism exposes its antihuman and, more specifically, anti-woman ideology. "Sthree Yoni/ Neecha Yoni/ Mlecha Yoni" are common contemptuous terms used to refer to the genitals of the mother/woman in relation to birth in Brahmanical texts and discourses, of which the *Gita* could be an iconic example, radically exposed by historians like D D Kosambi and Dalit theorists like Ilaiah[8]. More than antihuman and anti-woman it is strategically anti-Dalit Bahujan in the most extreme sense since it condemns common people as "Shudra Yoni and Neecha Yoni"(this is also a curse to the genitals of the gendered subaltern, the lower caste woman and the assumed lower status of the masses).[9] By taking the second ritualistic birth Brahmanism purges itself from the pollution of taking birth in the genitals of the mother/woman. Brahmans are superior to the masses who do not take the second birth, and are therefore worthy of their worship and service, so goes the discourse! But the hegemonic effect of this discourse that permeates the fabric of Indian society and culture all along the post Buddhist history is indeed disastrous.

The second superior birth that makes all the women and the subaltern the inferior other fetched Brahmanism its nationhood and its cultural geography. We might call it Hindu colonialism, a typical site of internal imperialism and hegemony. Thus Dalit Bahujans, the minorities and the women, the other of the Brahmanic imagination, have always remained outside the society and the nation, in both the pre- and post- colonial contexts of India. Path breaking attempts by the Bahujan theorists after Ambedkar, like Gopal Guru, have identified the growing hegemony in the contemporary state and civil society paradigms set up by the new and more aggressive advocates of the second birth, the top twice born, TTB as they are called[10]. The Brahmanic legacy of two births is now going national and international in the new fads of Vedic, Tantric and "exotically ethnic" eco-spiritual fantasies.[11]

Despite its depiction of the decadent and rotting state of Brahmanism and its parasitic social order, the text of *Samskara* reiterates the notion of Brahman-centered village/ world and nationhood with Shudra footmen to manipulate the masses and control the natural and "subhuman" resources of the nation. The subhumans or "Chandals" who are denied the human status are deprived of their very identity and are mere carcasses in the margins of Agraharas, villages and cultivable lands, "neither Brahmin nor shudra, but mere carcasses, stinking carcasses" in the margins of civilized existence. The gaps and silences in the representation of the real majority of the people make *Samskara* just another Brahmanic hegemonic text. It also becomes a hegemonic text in that it reasserts the patriarchal and hierarchical core of the Brahmanic worldview, reflected in the character of the protagonist, Praneshacharya, the high priest of Brahmanism in the Agrahara.[12] Though this "round" character undergoes a series of changes and transformations in and through socialization outside his Agrahara, we see that the antidemocratic and antihuman tenets of the Brahmanic worldview are reiterated and reinstalled in this character towards the end of the narrative.

The idea is quite explicit in the subtitle given by the translator, which suggests that it is the "Samskara" (in both senses as the "last rite" and "culture") of a man that becomes the central theme of the novel. The woman and her Samskara is far from the imagination of the writer/translator, and it is not inappropriate to conclude that the man in question is (Brah)man, rather than man in general. We know that even human status makes sense only within the limits of the Agrahara. Women and outcastes are obviously the lost folk who are denied the basic freedoms of equality, expression, public action and the last rites. The Agrahara women are denied the right to speak in public and before the men. Thus the patriarchal and anti-subaltern ideology of "BrahManism" is explicit from the very beginning.

In the Agrahara women are literally protected and controlled by men, as per the codes of Manu. Acharya's devotion to his bed-ridden wife too includes this problematic. He washes her body but washes himself to remove the pollution from talking to the Shudra woman, Chandri (1-2). It is not only the low castes who pollute but women of "superior birth" too are polluting to the Brahman. The woman of his own caste too is polluting in her periods, but though (Brah)men also have sexuality they are deemed to be eternally pure, unlike their own women. This is the purity-pollution riddle of BrahManism. If Brahman woman herself is polluting what is one to say about the outcastes and their women. Yet their body and labour are consumable under the cover of darkness and in disguise. See for instance the experiences of Belli and Chandri with Brahmanic males at night; and the story invoked within the text of Sankara's disguise for safe sex: "Sankara your great founder in his hunger for full experience exchanged his body for a dead king's and enjoyed himself with the queen, didn't he?"(6-7). This is only a sample of the double stance of BrahManism toward women, and subaltern women in particular. Look at the experience of Chandri the Shudra woman. The sin she committed was just to love a Brahman. "Chandri was Naranappa's concubine. If Acharya talked to her he would be polluted; he would have to bathe again before his meal" (2).

Naranappa the anti-Brahmanic Brahman of the Agrahara is dead and rotting in the Agrahara and the pollution of the lower caste woman is preventing his last rites: "Is he a real Brahmin at all, he slept regularly with the lowcaste woman [..]. A Brahmin isn't lost because he takes a lowborn prostitute [..]" (5). Thus goes the discourse of the inmates of the Agrahara regarding the purity-pollution issue. One thing is reiterated in the discourse, and it is that there are high and low births and the Brahman is of superior birth. Even drinking and eating meat comes only after low caste pollution (6). So it is not just life practice, but descent and birth too are mystified and connected to notions of religious and cultural superiority. The power of discourse operating in the Brahmanic patriarchal subordination and sexual exploitation of the subaltern women are central to the debate here. The subaltern is always blamed:

> 'This whore, this seducing witch! [...] if she had not given him potions why should he push aside his own kinswoman and throw all the ancestral gold and jewels on the neck of this evil witch!' (7)

So the lowcaste woman is a whore in the gaze of upper caste woman too. She is talked upon as seducing her male. Seductiveness of the subaltern is blamed and cursed while the real villain – patriarchal BrahManism - goes undetected.

If Brahmanic women see subaltern women as degraded and voluptuous creatures who pollute the "BrahMen," by assuming a cultural and moral policing position, it is interesting to note the BrahMen's own view of the low caste women:

> For the first time his connoisseur eyes had the chance to appraise this *precious object* which did not normally stir out of the house, this *choice object* that Naranappa had brought from Kundapura. A real *"sharp" type* exactly as described in Vatsyayana's manual of love- look at her, toes longer than the big toe, just as the love manual says, look at *those breasts*. In sex she is the type who *sucks the male dry*. Her eyes which should be fickle are now misty with grief and fear, but she looks good that way. Like Matsyagandhi the fisher woman in the Ravivarma print hung up in Durgabhatta's bedroom, shyly trying to hide her breasts bursting through her poor rag of a sari. The same eyes and nose: no wonder Naranappa threw away the worship stone for her, ate taboo meat and drank taboo liquor. One wonders at his daring. One remembers Jagannatha the Brahmin poet who married the Muslim girl, and his verses about the alien's breasts. If Praneshacharya were not present, if Naranappa wasn't lying dead right there, he would have happily quoted the stanza and expanded on it even to theses barren Brahmins. 'To the lustful'- that is Naranappa and his like- 'there is no fear, no shame' as the saying goes. (8-9)

One should pay special attention to the expressions used to describe the subaltern woman as mere sex object. Though she is untouchable and deadly polluting, her body contours are watering the high priests' mouth in lust. She is an object or commodity for his consumption. The pollution question is cleverly resolved by invoking the Matsyagandhi episode from the *Mahabharata*, where another high priest of Brahmanism violates an untouchable woman in a boat, under the cover of a mystical cloud. See how epic justification is summoned to legitimize this banal infatuation. Another reference brought in to make the register some what sexological and secularly erotic is that of Vatsyayana's *Kamasutra*, a sexist Brahmanic treatise that tells the high priests how to "enjoy" a woman. Interestingly, women can be categorized in to various morphological "types" according to this text. There is no mention of explicit caste specifications here, and this is done precisely to enlarge women's commodity status. Another reference is to Ravi Varma's notoriously docile feminine figures that enact the choreography of colonial modernity/masculinity in a pan Indian canvas of epic and mythological BrahManism.[13] All these instances of hegemonic gaze articulate the phallocentric and hierarchical worldview of Brahmanism that treats the subaltern/woman as a mere object of its order.

But even in such a decadent condition the anti-Brahmanic outcaste Naranappa's body is not allowed to be touched and cremated by low castes. Even in the most degraded form, the rotting body of a BrahMan should be made inaccessible to the untouchables. The politics of untouchability is nurtured on such painstaking endeavours.

> 'Only another Brahmin has any right to touch his body. If we let someone else to do it, we would be sullying our Brahmanhood. Yet I can't tell you go ahead with the rites. We all saw how he lived. What shall we do? What do the law books say?' (9)

Even Brahman women could not stand to see the dead body being touched by a lowcaste:

> Anasuya nagged him. 'Wasn't Naranappa my own maternal uncle's son? Sinner he may be. But if any lowcaste man is allowed to pick up his dead body, I'll die of shame.' (32)

The Brahman psyche itself is puzzling in these eternal paradoxes, yet it could not give up since power matters. This inherent contradiction of Brahmanism is again articulated by Acharya: "It is not truly brahmanical to get someone else to do what you don't do yourself" (13). Throughout its history, it should be remembered that Brahmanism as a social institution has utilized the Dalit Bahujans to do the menial and "polluting manual works" including that of lifting their excreta. Another internal riddle of the Brahmanic legacy, concerning "lowcaste" Brahmans, or Smartas, who are the out castes within Brahmanism, is again relevant here:

> The Parijatapura folk (Smartas) were unhappy over their friend's death, but quite *happy they were getting a chance to cremate a highcaste Brahmin*. They were pleased because Naranappa ate in their houses with no show of caste pride. (19)

The most striking thing here is that the Smartas are submissive to such hair splitting hierarchy, and are happy to get an opportunity to touch a dead uppercaste Brahman body. Such psychological subordination and subservient acceptance of hegemony is not visible elsewhere in history in any other power structures. The basic motifs of caste envy and greed that separate the caste strands in an eternal hierarchy of desire have been identified by scholars like P K Balakrishanan in the context of Kerala[14]. Brahmanism's peculiar blend of the social and the religious, the everyday and the metaphysical effected with the purpose of subordinating and exploiting the masses, has already been analyzed by Dalit theorists like Kancha Ilaiah.[15]

The superiority discourse of Brahmanism is based on a life of inhuman idealism and pedantic perversion driven by the principles of purity and pollution, the sacred birth and divine right theories, the semiotics of eating, dressing, social intercourse and spiritual obscurantism.[16] According to critics like Ilaiah, it represents a denial of the organic and the human in life and of being one with nature. It is a total negation of working culture and a disgrace to human labour and toil. It condemns work as "polluting" and cunningly feeds on the surplus of the masses parasitically. A sense of hierarchy is central to it.

Naranappa's life is a typical violation of all these Brahmanic virtues. That is why he is termed as the anti Brahmanic being of the Agrahara. He eats meat, drinks liquor, sleeps and mixes with low castes and outcaste women. He demystifies sacred stories and taboos. He leads a life of sensuous and organic fulfillment. He condemns the Brahmanic ideal of life denial and pedantic perversion (20-26).

Another important silence or gap in the text in relation to the central question of cleansing and the burial of the dead is the one relating to the "Chandals" and the Avarnas. As far as the text is concerned, they do not exist at all. Even Chandri is a Shudra, the lowest in the Savarna category. Thus the mass of Dalit Bahujans are simply out of the narrative discourse. Even a casual mention of the working communities may ruin and subvert the elite claims of Brahmanism as the sovereigns of the land and its hideous hegemony built upon religious and metaphysical obscurantism. The fundamental question of whether there was nobody to cultivate, cook and clean, gets cunningly and carefully suppressed in *Samskara*. The text is careful to avoid asking this vital question; some ideological constraints silence such an endeavour. Thus Brahmanism is not just a fascist tendency in nationalist discourses of all variety ranging from the national freedom movement to contemporary Hindutva politics and the pseudo-secularism of the Congress and the Left,[17] but an omnipresent and all-pervasive ideology in the cultural and socio-political discourses of literature; history, education, economics, development, the media, the cinema, music and pop culture. Here it would be worth referring to the Brahmanic camaraderie of Pillai and Nampoodiripadu in *The God of Small Things* for narrative instances of such double speak from the Left in the context of Kerala (see the fifth chapter).

The pedantry of life denial and the sublimated uses of chastity for social status and moral policing are other Brahmanic virtues enacted by Acharya in *Samskara*, though he fails pathetically in this precarious double game. This ridiculous contradiction is illustrated by his commentary on classical erotic couplets from Kalidasa. Naranappa accuses him of provoking and perverting the Brahman youth (only males are allowed this literary erotic enjoyment from the great, sacred classical epics):

> This man who speaks so beautifully about *Kalidasa's women*, does he feel any desire himself? Actually Shripati had taken Belli at the river when she had come to get water, only after he had heard the Acharya speak of *Shakuntala's beauty*. He couldn't stand it anymore. Belli was carrying a pitcher of water on her head, the rag on her body has slipped, and as *she stood in the moon light bouncing her breasts, the colour of earth-* she'd look like Shakuntala herself. He had then personally, carnally, enjoyed the Acharya's description. Tonight Shripati took an inside trail and walked straight to the outcaste hutments on the hillside. (39)

The classical Sanskrit erotica not just exoticizes the "earthen coloured breasts" of the subaltern woman but it also teaches how to consume it under cover. It is also important here to note that the whole of Sanskrit literature glorified and canonized by the nationalist discourses are explicitly anti-woman and anti-subaltern. In the epics the land and the body of the subaltern are to be conquered and consumed and kept under life-long slavery by the cultured/civilized/ Sanskritized masters. The male fantasies of the Brahmanic epics textualize the body of the subaltern as an obscure object of desire, to be violated and ordered and accommodated in the hegemonic epistemology by the highcaste male. Remember the Matsyagandhi episode from the *Mahabharatha* mentioned in the text (32). The text of *Samskara* inherits this Brahmanic "legacy" of writing the underdog and his/her body through the representations of Belli and Chandri, with their exoticized, eroticized and ready-to-consume bodies, with all the "follies and frailties of women."

So through Acharya, Kalidasa inspires Shripati to do the archetypal act of conquering the body and the mind of the subaltern, the essential hegemonic act of Brahmanism that ensured its sustenance from Vedic times onwards. Here it is vital to analyze the representation of Belli and her body in the text. As we have seen, it inherits the tradition of epic exoticism and classical erotica, true legacies of Brahmanism. The mention of Vatsyayana earlier on in the narrative too is important in this connection. The passage quoted above (39) plays with the eroticism of the land/body-scape, with its references to the moon light, riverbanks and bouncing earthy breasts. The text has no sympathy for the woman victim, and its description of the setting is so subtly and evocatively used to make it all appear natural and normal, a mere response to nature's call. Shripati's Brahmanhood is temporarily suspended since he is acting and digressing under cover and Kalidasa's "poetic justice" defends him through the sacred commentary of the Acharya. The ideology of the text is quite explicit here. There is nothing wrong in two humans meeting and copulating. The text cannot escape from its legitimization project of the highcaste male's violation of the subaltern woman. Where have all the purity-pollution questions gone? There is absolutely no concern shown for poor Belli, the lowcaste woman.

Thus the text not just remains silent about the subaltern existence and the struggle of the subaltern to survive, but it also tries desperately to erase and mute the cries and curses that come from underneath the conqueror's invading legs. It legitimizes the historic wrongs and injustices done by Brahmanism to the Dalit Bahujans and the subaltern communities, and mediates to make it all instinctual and "organic."

Another instance of legitimization and apologist representation is evident in Belli's taking for granted the low caste's poverty and slavery. Her epistemology and worldview is so amicably and smoothly compromising to Brahmanism's power requirements that there is no tension whatsoever among the communities even on the question of land and property issues. It is an instance of ventriloquism, where Manu speaks through the novelist Anantha Murthy. Belli's passive acceptance of the status quo and hegemony is her way of articulating her worldview:

> She had always been like ripe ears of corn bending before the falling rain. Belli wrapping the clothes around her said: 'Ayya, I want to tell you something, I 've never seen such a thing before. Why should rats and mice come to our poor huts? Nothing there to eat. Our huts aren't like Brahmin houses.' (40)

So it is natural that the Dalit woman bends before the Brahman male and normal that Dalit huts are ridden with poverty while the Brahman houses are overflowing with prosperity. So simple! The BrahMan is the lord and master of all he surveys, including the land and the living bodies that are created for his service by god!

But the problem receives clearer focus in the description of the BrahMan who can make sex with the low caste woman, but cannot talk to her: "Belli was alright for sleeping with; she was no good for talk. If she opens her mouth, she talks only ghosts and demons" (41). Bodies are useful not the brain and the tongues. Brahmanism views these other bodies not as human, but as animal. Mastering of such beastly land/body-scapes is again part of the superior Sanskritization/Hinduization discourse of Brahmanism. The brutality of this system is that not only talk and socializing are taboo in physical contact, but the subaltern has to stand self-cursedly at the lords' doorsteps for scraps of rotten food:

> Chinni begged standing at a distance: please avva throw a morsel for my mouth, avva. Sitadevi went in, brought out some betel leaf, threw them at her. Chinni tucking away the betel in her lap said. (58)

After all, Chinni is there to lift the whole family's excreta and to wash their toilet clean! Such inhuman conditions of living make these wretched of the earth resign to their fate and submissive to hegemony. They also nurture the hope of improving their position in the caste hierarchy someday. Chandri's desire for upward mobility in the caste hierarchy should be understood in this perspective. For a Shudra woman like Chandri even a touch of a Brahman is uplifting in these premises (67). For her class of Brahmanical subcastes of Shudras too "Chandals" are not humans, but mere beasts. The Shudra worldview too is limited within the poles of Brahman and Shudra, that is expressed in her realization that her lover is no longer present and only a stinking carcass remains, "neither Brahman nor shudra"(70). This exclusivist world could only be violated and trespassed by the Brahman male who can use any body in the touchable and untouchable categories. Consider the evaluation of body statistics of the low caste women by BrahManic youth: "They *measured and judged* all the lowcaste women" (73).

In the wet earth and in the warmth of the lowcaste woman (two peculiarly polluting things to Brahmanic high castes), Acharya the high priest of Brahmanic pedantry and asceticism discovers the organic and natural way of living, leaving behind his dying wife and the rotting Agrahara (80-85). Let us watch the Acharya coming out of the sex-slumber:

> Something occurred to him and he got up. Like an animal with his snout to the ground, he entered the woods where he made love to Chandri. Even in broad day light, it was shady and dusky there. In the bushes it was quite dark, a humming dark. He stood at the place where his life had turned over. The weight and shape of their bodies still visible on the green grass. He sat down. Like an idiot, he pulled out the blades of grass and smelled them. He had come from the death stench of the agrahara; the smell of grassroots smeared with wet earth held him in its power like an addiction. Like a hen pecking at and raking the ground, he pulled at everything that came to his hand and smelled it. (83)

A movement away from the inward-looking and narcissistic ideology and epistemology toward an organic epistemology that inculcates the growth and reproduction of the earthly beings and the virtues of the work culture could be identified easily in this passage. It seems to mark the beginning of Praneshacharya's second birth, that takes him out of his twice-born metaphysics. From here till the end the narrative presents the image of a wandering Brahman outside his agrahara. In his escapist bouts with Putta, an idler, outside his village the Acharya observes the world around and learns a lot about it. But even after his encounters with the outer world, his mind is disturbed to see lowcaste women. On seeing Padmavati he sweats, since she was a Malera, "a half caste woman"(122). But still he registers her bodily statistics:

> Acharya stood up and looked at Padmavati, long hair, not yet oiled after a bath, plump fleshy thighs, buttocks, breasts, tall, long limbed. A gleam in the eyes an expectation. A waiting. Must have a ritual bath in the river after her period. Breasts rise and fall as she breathes in and out. They will harden at the tips if caressed in the dark. (124-25)

At this advanced stage of the narrative there would not be any doubt about the real transformations of this character. He is still the personification of caste/gender prejudices and its divided worldview. Even after his intimate sexual relations with the low caste woman Chandri, his sexist attitude towards women and the world in general has not changed. Even after experiencing the decadence of rotting Brahmanism, his caste consciousness and pollution-phobia persist. As an icon and victim of Varnadharma this BrahMan cannot become a man. Or his BrahManism makes its second coming or rebirth even after his organic initiation in to the human way of living. He is "twice-born" in the sense that he takes his second birth into an exclusionary world of pseudo-superiority based on religious and metaphysical obscurantism and ideological exploitation through the instrument of caste and perpetuates the power discourses of hegemony.

At this point the real question of giving up cultural superiority and social hegemony has been apologetically concealed and marginalized in the text with an equation that says either Brahmanism or chaos: "Unless I shed brhmanhood altogether I cannot stand aside, liberated from all this, if I shed it, I'll fall into the tigerish world of cock-fights" (130-31). This apology for the rebirth, this characterization of the non-Brahmanic Dalit Bahujan cultures and worldviews as mere "cock-fight," its essential contempt for the basic communities and their work cultures can hardly conceal Brahmanism's fear of the loss of hegemony.

Things are not much different in Rao Bahaddur's *Gramayana* which is also set in another good old South Indian village. The Karnataka village in *Gramayana* could easily pass for the marginalized other of the urban Indian city-centre. But a close look at this narrative of the village mythology would expose the hollowness of the reductionist dichotomy. It reveals the plight of the really marginalized and eternally subjected within this so called periphery, problematizing the whole debate of rural, subaltern post coloniality manifesting along caste and gender lines. Padalli is a typical "caste-swaraj" Indian village with its inscribed and unwritten constitution of caste hierarchy, life long bonded slavery and gender oppression.[18] Patriarchy and Brahmanic priesthood operate here in tandem in order to squeeze and victimize the lower castes and women in general. The picture of the sexed subaltern is worse.

As is the case with the history of all Indian villages, Padalli's history has been appropriated or hijacked by Sanskrit Brahmanic consolidation and nomenclature.[19] It, according to sacred legend originates from Parasurama Padalli(village). And no doubt Brahmins were its chosen owners! Colonialism, kingship and feudalism, along with Brahmanic priesthood and cultural monopoly, choke the land (1-3).[20] The mansion of Jagirdar, the male head of the village, cleric Kulkarni, priest Acharyar and Brahmanic monk Padadappa along with a series of royal police men literally constitute the patriarchal frame work of the village. Chimana, the sister of Dada, the central figure, becomes the victim of this illegitimate collusion between patriarchy and priesthood. Hundreds of outcastes who live on the margins of the village form the basic working class and the fundamental victims of this economy. The river Krishna forms the backdrop of this agrarian society and finally washes off the margins to doom. Even after this holocaust the master-slave relation and hierarchy is reestablished and caste disequilibrium is re-balanced through Kariappa showing signs of the beginning of a new era of life long slavery in the fields, a typical revival and reestablishment of hegemony. This reinstating and reinforcing of the hegemonic world view and the ancient antihuman power relations makes *Gramayana* a subservient text of the dominant Brahmanical ideology.

Pulaya, shepherd and cobbler slums are the real margins of this village. They are outside the great entrance of the village and their settlements, movement, speech and activity are restricted and they face the threat of being further pushed to the periphery by the floods. The narrative mentions them always with a caste prefix unlike the Savarna lords with surnames and other tales and titles. The sex workers of the village are exclusively from the Pulaya slum. The Pulayas are in charge of taking the carcasses to the periphery of the village for burial. All other menial jobs as well as productive work are their 'natural' duty.[21]

The narrative adds abusive epithets to the outcastes like "Madigar" and "cobbler." Their women are mere sex objects and nothing more than "whores." See this typical female/ subaltern representation: "His (Channna's) sister, that *slut* Malli who is left for the service of God was also there with the end of her saree in her teeth, swaying her hips, and peeping from behind the conrner" (149). The village "whores" are exclusively confined to the subaltern slums. Chandri is a typical Devadasi (242). (See pages 243-44 for an elaborate "whore" representation.) This exclusionary and contradictory nature of the Pulaya slum and Padalli village provides a striking parallel between the caste ethics of Varnasrama Hinduism and its social manifestation of pandemonium, in the experience of the basic working castes and communities.

When the famine strikes the village because of the hoarding of grains by the upper castes, the Dalits become the real victims of it. They starve to death, they fall prey to the poisoned and decayed maize that was given away at the time of calamity.

The untouchables were merely exploited by the Brahmanic monk Padadappa and mobilized for illegal and criminal acts at this critical juncture of calamity. Their thinking and action, everything is controlled and manipulated from the top, that is from the Brahman head, exactly as the Varnasrama ideology demands. They address the upper castes as "master/lord" and consider it their duty and privilege to serve and die for the feudal lords and caste superiors: Pulaya Rudra says to the lords: "O master we are mere pebbles in your hands" (232).

It is not only the outcastes and Dalits who are misrepresented in the narrative. Members of minority religions too are presented as grotesque and comic/ridiculous in the rustic village saga that exposes the xenophobia and hatred of the other in traditional Hindu societies and villages. Jain Jinnappa is always frugal, eccentric, and useless. He is the butt of ridicule in the narrative (274-87).

The female representations of the narrative explicitly assert the patriarchal and oppressive gender balance of such societies. All the women are subservient to their "lords" (husbands). Chimana is the typical victim of patriarchy and Brahmanic priesthood. She was molested and ruined by Padadappa the priest, the head of the Hindu monastery in the village. But the remarkable point is that from the moment of losing her "chastity" she is condemned to live a degraded life by her own brother, the heroic protagonist Dada. The response of the villagers to her victim-hood is even worse. She is forced to spend her life ever after with Padadappa in his monastery, which is the den of drug addicts and perverted escapists. To resist the advances of Lingappa, a stooge of Padadappa, she immolates herself, leaving the child born in wedlock, an orphan. She is only a representative of women suffering under Hindu patriarchy in such good old rural Gram-swarajs.[22]

Though the narrative reflects the harsh realities of patriarchy, corrupt and hellish priesthood and caste hierarchy in the village, it assumes a detached neutral tone, rather than a polemical one. The notions of caste hierarchy and the subhuman plight of the outcastes are acknowledged by the text as normal and natural.

Another aspect of the narrative is the preponderance in it of descriptions concerning upper caste households and characters, and specifically of men from such environment. Men are the central figures in the narrative as well as in the village, despite the fact that the work they do is nothing more than gossip, sex and pooja; of course, they are the ones who hoard and consume the grains produced by the working communities. Balacharyar, the Brahmanic priest, is a typical example. Acharyar occupies the central position in the socio-cultural and religious realms of the village, like Praneshacharya in *Samskara*. The narrative, especially in the latter half, meanders around him. The omniscient narrative is tempted too often to adopt the "reserved and reverent" perspective of the "mature" Brahmanic patriarch, as the finale of floods approaches. Another important feature is that for onward motion and linear as well as lateral progression of the plot the narrative pushes on with the upper caste households and characters and the multitudes of outcastes are mere pawns in the hands of the caste Hindus, but they are fated to face the calamities of the lords' handiwork, whether it be floods, famine or epidemic. Actually it is the parasitic existence of the caste Hindus that complicates the economic equations of the village that is visited frequently by epidemics like malaria and plague. Food poisoning and starvation deaths too are the result of the misrule of the caste lords.

But the narrative places a metaphysical and fundamental oppressive text that theorized caste system - the *Gita* - in the hands of Acharyar to kindle a spark of hope and survival at this advanced stage of wreckage. Only revivalist Hindu solutions are sought for this fundamental flaw in the system. The suggested path of mystic and religious revival instead of rational enquiry in confronting economic and social issues leads to further ruins. But unfortunately the sufferers in greater quantity form the outcastes on the periphery. But their tragedy is not even fully mentioned. The narrative focuses on the impact of the rain and floods on the caste Hindus, especially on the Acharyar family. Even in death the outcastes are anonymous and are outside the boundaries of the village that survived for generations on their labour, as well as outside the margins of the narrative that carefully or conveniently represses the people's greater calamity.[23] This is a typical instance of the ideological avoidance of the fundamental labour and productive culture in the narratives that boast about portraying the "culture" of the rural, "self sufficient" Indian-Hindu villages. The masses on whose toil and hardship the nation survives are always out side the margins of discourse. Whenever cultural discourses talk about margins they are playing the double game of avoiding and muting the real margin, the original subaltern, from the discourse and replacing the imagiNation and fiction with their favourite caste Hindu Acharyars and their henchmen. The real inhabitants and owners of the land, the productive castes and classes, are sidelined in such narratives.

Continuing with this upper caste affiliation the narrative of *Gramayana* goes on to add that while thousands merely "die" in the floods, Acharyar enters "Jalsamadhi"! It too is unforgettable that even amidst epidemics like plague all kinds of manual and menial work are carried out by the Dalits: Pulaya Rudra is asked to set fire to the uppercaste household after the family dies of plague. The subalterns are forced to do the burial as well as sanitation among the epidemic-infested households. While upper caste Hindus enjoy the advantage of higher topographic location in the village, the outcastes of the margin are washed away by the rising waters of the flooding Krishna.

But what is most remarkable is the end of the novel. Even after the extensive natural calamities that killed thousands and literally swept away the Padalli village, the new dawn after this purgation presents a renewed master-slave "organic" bond. Dada the caste Hindu lord and Kariappa the Pulaya slave are back and "naturally" the slave reasserts his loyalty to the young caste lord: "Am I not serving my master [..] as long as I live"(595). That reiterates the whole story. The hierarchy is thus reestablished, the power structures remain intact, and there is no threat to the status quo. No end to caste/gender hierarchy and hegemony. The unending saga of the Indian village goes on.

Notes

1. The *Gita* verse beginning "Chaturvarnyam Mayasrushtam..." and the *Manusmruti* could form fundamental references here.
2. See Sumit Sarkar, "Indian Nationalism and the Politics of Hindutva," *Making India Hindu*, ed. Ludden D (New Delhi: Oxford UP, 1997) and *Beyond Nationalist Frames: Post Modernism, Hindu Fundamentalism, History* (Bloomington: Indiana UP, 2002) for detailed explications of the Brahmanical imagination of the Indian nation with its typical "others" and outcastes. Also see Sundar Sarukkai, "The Other in Anthropology and Philosophy," *Economic and Political Weekly* 32 (1997):1406-09, that affirms the validity of fiction as an important tool for socio cultural and ethnographic data and a fundamental epistemological site. The notion of the politics of fiction as related less to the thematic content and more to the ideological connotations it acquires in the process of reading in material discursive contexts, and the idea of generic and intrinsic affiliation of fiction to the dominating/hegemonic ideology in a given society are perspectives extended from P P Raveendran, "Politics in the Malayalam Novel: A Reading of C R Parameswaran's Prakrutiniyamam," *Indian Literature* 38, 5 (1995): 156-59. Also see Susie Tharu "Refiguring Literary/Cultural Historiography," *Economic and Political Weekly* 33 (1998): 1508-09, and V Geetha and S V Rajadurai, "Neo Brahmanism: An Intentional Fallacy," *Economic and Political Weekly* 28 (1993): 129-36.
3. U. R. Ananta Murthy, *Samskara, A Rite for a Dead Man*, trans. A K Ramanujan (New Delhi: Oxford UP, 1996) 150.
4. See Satish Deshpande, "Communalising the Nation-space: Notes on Spatial Strategies of Hindutva," *Economic and Political Weekly* 30 (1995): 3220-27, for an elaborate account of the Neo Brahmanical spacing strategies in post Independent India. Also see his "Hegemonic Spatial Strategies: The Nation Space and

Hindu Communalism in Twentieth Century India," *Subaltern Studies XI: Community, Gender and Violence,* ed. Partha Chatterjee and Pradeep Jeganathan (New Delhi: Permanent Black, 2000) where he identifies the various ways in which Hindutva tries to redefine the nation space through rearticulating the link between an imagined community and its territorial domain, concluding by looking at Hindutva and globalization as spatial strategies.

5. Meenakshee Mukherjee, *Realism and Reality: The Novel and Society in India* (New Delhi: Oxford UP, 1985) 166-78.

6. For a brilliant analysis of the perverted and exploitative aspects of Brahmanism see Uma Chakravarti, "Conceptualizing Brahmanical Patriarchy in Early India: Gender, Caste, Class and State," *Economic and Political Weekly* 28 (1993): 579-85; where she identifies caste hierarchy and gender hierarchy as the organizing principles of the Brahmanic power structure.

7. See *Manudharma Sastra*, or *Laws of Manu,* trans. George Buhler (Delhi: M B D, 1984) for the notorious "Sanatana Laws" of Brahmanism.

8. See D D Kosambi, *Myth and Reality* (Malayalam Trans.), ed. Rajan Gurukkal (Calicut: Jansakti, 1989) 51-80; specifically the section "Socio Economic Aspects of the Gita," for a detailed analysis of the economic and political functions that the *Gita* served for the Brahmanic hegemony in India. Kosambi exposes the irrational nature of the discourses of Brahmanism and the role of the Krishna figure in securing ideological subordination and consent construction from the masses. Kosambi also identifies the affinity of the Brahmanic leaders of Indian nationalism (Tilak, Gandhi and Patel) to the text of *Gita* and their various appropriations and interpretations of it, reiterating its canonical status. The legacy of this hegemonic hermeneutics can also be traced back to Sankara, Ramanuja, Jnanesvar and Aurobindo. For a discussion of the Brahmanic revisionist intervention in the epics and popular cults, see "The Possible Sources of the Gita," *Combined Methods in Indology and Other Writings: D D Kosambi*, ed. B Chathopadhyaya (Delhi; Oxford UP, 2002) 373-90.

9. Luce Irigary, "The Power of Discourse and the Subordination of the Feminine," *Literary Theory: An Anthology*, ed. Julie Rivkin and Michel Ryan (London: Routledge, 2000) 34-53. Gayatri Spivak's notion of the gendered subaltern could form a theoretical basis for the debate on this question carried out in the Indian context of Brahmanism by scholars like Veena Pooncha, "Why Women Fear Religious Fundamentalism: Hindutva's Hidden Agenda," *Economic and Political Weekly* 28 (1993): 438-39; Susie Tharu and T Niranjana, "Caste and the Gendered Body," *Economic and Political Weekly* 31 (1996): 1311-15; Sharmila Rege, "Dalit Women Talk Differently: A Critique of Difference and Towards a Dalit Feminist Stand Point Position," *Economic and Political Weekly* 33 (1998): 39-46; Rajeswari Sunder Rajan, "Is the Hindu Goddess a Feminist," *Economic and Political Weekly* 33 (1998): 34-38 and *Real and Imagined Women: Gender, Culture, Post colonialism* (London: Routledge, 1998).
10. See Gopal Guru, "How Egalitarian are the Social Sciences in India?" *Economic and Political Weekly* 37 (2002): 5003-09, for a brilliant analysis of the "epistemological imperialism" of the academy and the social science practices in India by the TTB (top twice born). For a comprehensive survey of the material manifestation of caste hierarchy and hegemony throughout the Indian public sphere and state apparatuses, see Andre Beteille, "Caste in Contemporary India," *Equality and Universality: Essays in Social and Political Theory* (New Delhi: Oxford UP, 2002) 178-86.
11. The perpetual reductionism/avoidance/silence and a sort of apology for caste-consciousness and a tactic foregrounding of the "tribal" appearing in the contemporary celebrated eco authors like Vandana Shiva and Ramanchandra Guha could be referred to here. See Ramachandra Guha, *An Ecological History of India* (New Delhi: Oxford UP, 2002).
12. Kancha Ilaiah, *Why I am not a Hindu: A Shudra Critique of Hindutva Culture, Ideology and Political Economy* (Calcutta: Samya, 1996) 26-28. See the chapter "Brahmanism as Patriarchy."
13. G Arunima, "Face Value: Ravi Varma's Portraiture and the Project of Colonial Modernity," *Indian Economic and*

Social History Review 40, 1 (2003): 57-80. This paper explores the portrait genre as the modular form in Ravi Varma's oeuvre, and pursues the question of modernity in his art. It argues that unlike the other artists of nineteenth century India, his modernity is not a product of 'critique' but of a different negotiation with both tradition and the west without even slightly disturbing patriarchal and hierarchical hegemonies.

14. P K Balakrishnan, *Jativyavastitiyum Kerala charithravum* (Kottayam: NBS, 1986). Balakrishan explores the socio cultural and economic history of Kerala along with the history of the caste system and explicates the desire and envy that is peculiar and central to the sustenance of caste in a hierarchical form, with each caste nurturing this desire and envy for the upper caste and contempt for the lower caste. Poets like Kumaran Asan too had pointed out the envious core of the caste earlier on in the initial decades of the twentieth century in the context of the Kerala renaissance.

15. See Kancha Ilaiah, *Why I am not a Hindu? A Shudra critique of Hindutva Culture, Ideology and Political Economy*, (Calcutta: Samya, 1996). Also see his "Brahmanism vs Dalitism: The Epistemological Conflict in History," *Cultural Subordination and the Dalit Challenge: Dalit Identity and Politics*, ed. Ghanshyam Shah (New Delhi: Sage, 2001) 108-128.

16. For a comprehensive account on the purity pollution riddles of Brahmanism, see Ghanshyam Shah, introduction, *Caste and Democratic Politics in India* (New Delhi: Permanent Black, 2003) 5-27.

17. Gail Omvedt, "Pseudo Secularism," *The Hindu* 20 &21 January 2003, exposes the hidden Brahmanic and Hindutva ideologies in operation in the National movement, in the Congress and in the Communist Marxist Left. Kancha Ilaiah also points to the disguised and hence more dangerous attitude of the left in "Brahmanism vs Dalitism: The Epistemological Conflict in History," quoting Kanshi Ram that BJP is a green snake in white grass, while the CPM is a green snake in green grass. M N Srinivas's less celebrated essay "Gandhi's Religion" also registers the contradictions in

Gandhi's choice of the *Gita* and his doctrine of non violence; see M N Srinivas, "Gandhi's Religion" *Economic and Political Weekly* 30 (1995): 376.

18. "Caste-Swaraj" is a contextual inversion of Gandhi's "Gram Swaraj," a construction that foregrounds its compromises with Brahmanic patriarchy and its historic betrayal of Bahujans, by legitimizing Varnadharma and caste Hindutva. See M K Gandhi, *Varnasramadharma* (Bombay: Navjeevan, 1962).

19. For example, consider the notorious legend of the sixty four Brahman villages of Kerala and the myth of Parasurama creating Kerala by just throwing his axe across the ocean. This hegemonic myth survives in twenty first century Kerala, in the guise of the Sanskritized naming of public properties and strategic spaces, as in the "Parasuram Express." Whether it is trains, toilets or universities, all of them carry Brahmanic Sanskritic names. Even in Kerala, a state that has achieved universal literacy and high human development standards; through subaltern anti caste movements and missionary efforts, one would come across universities in the names of Sankara and Gandhi but a university in the name of Ayyankali, Appachan or even Narayana Guru is a remote possibility. This itself is a typical instance of hegemony growing in the public sphere and polity even in the twenty first century. We know about the decades-long struggle that preceded the renaming of Marathwada University as Ambedkar University in Maharashtra. For a detailed account of the neo Brahmanic/Savarna naming strategies in the Kerala context see B R P Bhaskar, "Kavyabhavanayum Charithrasatyavum," *Kalakaumudi Weekly* 1264 (1999): 43-45.

20. Rao Bahaddur, *Gramayana*, trans. P V Joshi (New Delhi: Sahitya Akademi, 2002).

21. See Kancha Ilaiah, "Cow and Culture," *The Hindu*, 25 October 2002, for a detailed analysis of the polluting duties of Bahujans in India, and the role of the Brahmanic double speak in making them polluting. Ilaiah's essay also throws light on the persistence of the exploitation in several parts of present-day India. Also see S Anand, "Thyagaraja's Cow," *Outlook* 35 (2003): 58-9, that subverts the sanctity of Indian classical music, especially Carnatic music, that has been patronized and monopolized by

Brahmanism. Anand points out that the sound of the mridangam is the outcome of Dalit Bahujan leather craftsmen and that "mridangam cant be mridangam sans cow hide." The irony is that Brahmins who are the "most touchy" about the cow's divinity have to run their fingers on a slaughtered cow's hide to produce music.

22. Actually throughout its history Brahmanism in south India has not only used the muzzle power of Bahujans to expand the Varna social system, but has exploited their sexuality too to build the caste-swaraj villages. For example in Kerala they constituted sexual colonies among the Shudra women. See P. K. Balakrishnan, *Jativyavastayum Kerala Charithravum* (Kottayam: NBS, 1986) and Robin Jeffrey, *The Decline of Nayar Dominance: Society and Politics in Travancore; 1847-1908* (New York: Macmillan, 1976). The sexual act too has immense significance in constituting hegemony. The sexual act is a site for gender/cultural domination of the male and for the proving of "biological" and physical superiority, as Maurice Godelier argues in "What is a Sexual Act?," *Anthropological Theory* 3. 2 (2003): 179-98. Even after centuries things are not much different in India; for example see the patriarchal and Brahmanic core of the Left who are supposed to be sensitive to gender issues, articulated by Biswamoy Pati, "Women, Rape and the Left," *Economic and Political Weekly* 26 (1991): 219-20.

23. Typical narrative instances of the selection of premises, foregrounding and back grounding are attributives of the propaganda model of the power groups, say Noam Chomsky and Edward Herman, *Manufacturing Consent: The Political Economy of the Mass Media* (London: Vintage, 1994) Preface xv; "Observable pattern of indignant campaigns and suppressions, of shading and emphasis, and of selection of context, premises, and general agenda is highly functional for established power and responsive to the needs of major power groups."

4

Community and the Tribal : *Thalamurakal, Mavelimantam*

> Like a viper caste retreated in to the darkness of sleepy memories. (*Thalamurakal* 150)

> It is the lords who robe us, and it is the lords who unrobe us...
>
> What is there in a slave's body that the lords have not seen? (*Mavelimantam* 130)

O V Vijayan's *Thalamurakal* (Generations) has been widely read as a fictional attempt to recreate the history of caste society, bringing out its ironic subtleties and eternal paradoxes. It narrativizes the intricacies and complexities of the Varna- caste system under the hegemonic ideology of Brahmanism as manifested in the lifelong struggles of the inquisitive and rebellious male generations of the Ponmudi household in the Palghat region of Kerala. In their critical confrontation with caste, generations of men from this family struggled with their individual game plans that included conversion, Sanskritization and upward exogamy. The Sanskrit scholarship and "Brahmanyam" of Krishnan Uncle and the defiant conversions of Gopalan (Imtiaz) and Chamiarappan (Theodore) respectively to Islam and Christianity proved futile and absurd. The seductions of Brahmanism, the quest to achieve it and the futility of achieving it as well as the change in faith, everything is enacted in the continuous struggle of the members of the Ponmudi household. The central character Chandran, the grandson of Chamiarappan marries a German woman,

Rosemary Wagner, and their son Theodore Vel Wagner survives the struggle and curse of generations, as a racial hybrid who exceeds and endures caste.

As the novel opens the young Chandran is struggling with the hegemonic aspects of *Valmiki Ramayanam* in the Ponmudi tharavadu (7).[1] The opening chapter itself is named "Rama Banam" meaning the arrow of Rama, who is the Aryan God and the iconic protector of Varnadharma and the caste system and the executioner of Shambuka, the Shudra sage. Chandran wonders how the tribal Valmiki could sing the story of the elite Rama, a story that subtly evokes the history of Brahmanic ideological invasion and the sociological process of the tribes getting reorganized into castes. The suggestion obviously is to the ongoing processes of Sanskritization and Hinduization.

At this stage young Chandran is aware of the caste identity - the Avarna Ezhava identity - of his household. He is also aware of the conversion of his grand father Chamiarappan into Christianity as Theodore, following the torture at the Kalpathy Sathyagraham by Brahmans.[2] His young friend Chelly, the Dalit boy, tells him that Rama killed the Dalit Bahujans like Shambuka who tried to learn Sanskrit and that is why he is also afraid of going to school (8). Thus the long history of the denial of educational, economic, cultural as well as human rights to the vast majority of Dalit Bahujans in India under the hegemonic ideology of Brahmanism is evoked here as a contemporary question. Chelly also hates his very name that reminds him of these age old fears and injustices and Chandran has no hesitation whatsoever in rechristening him "Jesus Christ" after his rationalist grandfather's defiant praxis. Chandran also raises basic questions about caste identities before his grandfather (8).

Krishnan Uncle was the youngest brother of Chamiarappan's grandfather. His quest for Sanskrit and Brahmanic knowledge was a valorous attempt to explore, expose and disseminate the epistemological enigmas and knowledge/power monopolies endemic to Hinduism. Using his own community's limited knowledge of Ayurveda and astrology as a launching pad he strives to gain mastery over Brahmanic scholarship. He ventures out to Kashi/Banaras with a borrowed sacred thread from a colleague and arrives at the understanding of the futility of Brahmanic knowledge, that has deteriorated in to a hegemonic hermeneutics and epistemology within its protective codes like *Manusmruti*.

> Moving away from his caste occupation he studied Sanskrit poetry and grammar. It was the time of the reign of *Manusmruti*. His gurus couldn't quench his thirst for Sanskrit. Then it happened – the acquaintance with Chathunni Vaidiar. As an exception to Chathurvarnyam, in central Kerala there were some Avarna Vaidyar (practitioners of indigenous medicine, especially Ayurveda) families who were also Sanskrit scholars. Chathunni Vaidyar belonged to such a tradition. For the Avarna Vaidyars (physicians) the patient's caste was no bar. They could touch, caress and heal. There was no pollution and defilement as they applied the Dhanwanthari oil. In the hands of these Aswini Devas Sanskrit became herbal pastes and saffron for healthy generations. In the hands of Brahman it stagnated into cunning purity-pollution riddles [..] 'Beyond the writing and articulation of Sanskrit I want the world to know that an untouchable who holds *Brahmanyam* could do whatever a Namboodiri wearing a sacred thread is capable of' [...] Breaking his silence Chathunni Vaidyar said. 'Sanskrit is not the language of the Aryan, nor do theVedas and the Upanishads belong to him. Flesh eating rapist, nomadic Aryan couldn't have sung 'Neti, Neti', 'Chathurvarnyam Mayasrushtam' this is not *Gita*, invading some small human race on the verge of extinction he indoctrinated their sacred texts with the venom of his selfishness and arrogance.' These words of Chathunni Vaidyar led the curiosity of Krishnan Uncle to the Indus-Gangetic planes where reclined the history of the Aryan invasion and the Dravidian retreat. (13-14)[3]

So it was an intellectual and cultural challenge for Krishnan Uncle. His inquisitive spirit and explorative potential were the metaphoric articulation of the search of various colonized and marginalized people, the struggles of generations to regain their lost human rights and egalitarian dignity. In this historic enquiry the keen insights and critical observations of Chathunni Vaidyar influenced him deeply. Vaidyar himself is influenced by the changes in the power structures. He is aware of the "white lords" and their lord Jesus Christ , "a down trodden carpenter" of the old Roman empire, who cured common people of their afflictions by his touch (14).

> Jesus Christ was not a white man but brown like us. A poor carpenter who earned a living with his hands [..]. Our people have also begun learning foreign tongues. In Kongunadu and in south Venadu depressed castes follow this master carpenter of Nazareth. (15)

The history of colonial intervention and the option of conversion are brought in at this early stage of the narration. For the lower castes in Kerala conversion has been an option ever since the missionary intervention in the eighteenth century.[4] This was a kind of "touching cure" that shook the foundations of Brahmanism and provided an alternative worldview:

> It concerns memory, not the lack of it. The caste hegemonic attitude lying deep in the mind. That sees others as degraded and untouchable. Cure without mercy rendered the *Ashtangahrudaya* dry. Herbs and roots shrunk under the green. Let us return to Christ. When the diseased followed him he touched them, with out hesitation and contempt and gave them back their life and health. In the hands of the Namboodiris Ayurveda is mere verse... (16)

The knowledge/power monopolies and their controlled use for social engineering and dominance are suggested here. How tribal/folk forms of knowledge like indigenous medicine, integrated into Brahmanic epistemology metamorphose into the hegemonic instrument of governmentality becomes explicit here. The emancipatory touch that Jesus offers is just the opposite of this. This healing touch was a great gesture toward the elimination of caste in our cultural history, but unfortunately the Brahmanic fear of pollution still survives in disguise in all religions in the land. There are only Caste Hindus, Caste Christians, Caste Muslims, Caste Sikhs ...in India.[5]

The sense of supremacy and the fear of the loss of hegemony have been in operation in all these knowledge/ power discourses:

> The learned are hoarding the Sanskrit language. That is the fortress of violence. Remember the story of Ekalavya. There that divine language lay dying. We could have revitalized it, if only our Brahmans had not stood in the way. (18)

Krishnan Uncle's quest should be read and accommodated in this broader perspective. This is not an infatuation for Brahmanism, but a great redeeming endeavour of epic proportions. That is why he asks for the old sacred thread of his Brahman friend, rather than going for a new one. "I could have bought a new thread, but I need one that had experienced the futility of Brahmanism, a thread that is soaked in the futile sweat of a futile life sans good deeds. My intention is to redeem it" (19). But later in the narrative we find that this quest in to the treasure house of the Sanskrit/Brahmanic tradition also ends up in futility in Kashi where he curses the *Manusmruti* before his final exit.

Through the intimate and subtle portrayal of this scholar and his search the narrative problematizes the history and the present of the ideology of Sanskritization. It precariously articulates the paradoxes and puzzles in this social process and provides a critique of this urge for "upward" social mobility. This is important in contemporary India's social milieu, especially in the context of the orchestrated campaign for Hinduization and homogenization of Bahujans and Adivasis that are being launched by the dominant groups in India to achieve hegemonic and fascist goals.[6]

The question of Hinduization is again hinted at in the development of the Bali myth by Chandran in his identification with the racial experience of his German partner Rosemary Wagner. The cultural question of caste is given a global dimension by juxtaposing it with the ethnic and racial cleavages in Europe, especially in the period of the holocaust. The extermination of one human race by another is juxtaposed in Chandran's conscience with the subordination and marginalization of one group of people by another, epitomized in the myth of Maha Bali, the old Subaltern leader of south India, who was undone by the cunning of Vamana, the incarnation of Vishnu. The correspondence between Rosemary's father's refusal to kill Jews and Chandran's father's acquittal of young revolutionaries against official orders vitalizes this cross-cultural identification:

> The holy tale of the retreat and reemergence of Maha Bali. The subaltern emperor, the loving barbarian, the just ruler. The Vedic Brahmans say that Vishnu reincarnated as Vamana, not to bless these good virtues but to eliminate them. Poor slaves and peasants worship Vamana by erecting the mud idols of Bali. It was in the form of a pyramid. Broader base and pointed head, the humility of the Neanderthal man...in the run up to evolution and progress he sought the peace of the under world. That is the tale of Bali and Vamana distorted in and through time...Neanderthal man, Neanderthal emperor, the Paraya emperor who found peace in the depths of the earth. In the violence of evolution Maha Bali melted and sunk deep in to the underworld. His return shows the merging of the beliefs of the Aryan and the Dravidian. (27)

The invocation of the Bali myth has been central to several Dalit Bahujan rearticulations of history including those of Phule and Periyor.[7] It could also be found in narratives like *Mavelimantam*, (K J Baby's novel in Malayalam voicing the tribal question in Wayanadu, discussed later in this chapter) as an articulation of a subversive and counter-hegemonic desire, a primal myth of survival and resistance. In *Thalamurakal* it is also given a universal and simultaneously local dimension by calling Bali subaltern, barbarian, Neanderthal and Paraya at the same time. The Parayas belong to one of the earliest human settlers of the peninsula and are the most widely and abundantly distributed caste category through out South India. The epithet "the Paraya emperor" points towards the counter movement of Sanskritization enacted by Krishnan Uncle, as well as toward Dalitization dramatized in the Paraya alliance of Pavithran, the elder son of Chamiarappan, in the Tholannur Paraya slum, to be narrated later. But this pilot epithet provides a striking reconnection to the reader only when this unusual episode is exposed at an advanced state in the narrative.

From this myth of merging, Chandran and Rosemary move to the tentative solution of the racial amalgam and the notion of the redeeming hybrid child as a way out of the eternal labyrinth of caste and race. It also takes the form of an earnest plea for ethnic merging and exogamy reminding us of the doctrines of Dalit Bahujan thinkers like Ambedkar.[8]

> Only a hybrid child could save us from this crisis, a pure offspring of lust...let the *Gita* and the Furor bunker shiver in the rhythms of our union. (28)

The strategic role of the *Gita* in the perpetuation and legitimization of Brahmanic hegemony and its Varna system has been reiterated in the narrative, exposing its anti-Bahujan ideological history. Along with the *Manusmruti* it served as the key text that prohibited Varna mixing and

Bahujan learning for centuries and legitimized Caste as god given.

This caste regime in its total manifestation is narrativized in the tale of Sumati grandma whose humiliation by a caste lord in the field reveals the inhuman perversions of purity and pollution and of "caste distance" ('Shudrappadu' and 'Ezhavappadu'):

> Something forced her to obey the shouting. Through the long tunnel of five millennia that command pierced her ears. The decree and command of Caste. Unable to defend it she began her retreat. One Ezhavappadu, fourteen feet. Her eyes on her feet, Nair's on her bouncing breasts. With the fourteenth count she fell backwards into the muddy field. (29)

This common experience of shame and injustice unites the untouchable Ezhavas and Pulayas in solidarity against the Savarna caste-lords. Pangelappan, the father of Sumati, and his Pulaya assistant Rakkanakan join hands to avenge this disgrace:

> We both are in this same mud, we must wash this off. You are my brother from now on. (30)

This broader alliance and brotherhood has initiated social transformation in the land. The common experience of caste injustice has acted as the force that has strengthened today's Dalit Bahujan alliance. The non economic characteristic of caste is again developed in the episode of Sivakamy, the Brahman concubine of Appu Karanavar. There was no deficiency of wealth and prosperity for him, but still he felt something was missing. It was not the economic capital but the symbolic and cultural ones. So he literally bought a Brahmin concubine and tried to learn the Gayatri mantra from her. But his uncouth tongue and other speech organs failed him (31-2). This episode also provides a critique of orthodox Marxist positions regarding the economic category of class as the sole site of inequality and exploitation. It foregrounds the cultural and social materiality of caste and its non-economic contexts and their genealogy.

If Appu Karanavar failed to reconcile caste with economic and material power, Krishnan Uncle too was a total failure in his experiments with cultural, educational and symbolic capitals provided by Brahmanic and Vedic knowledge. He throws away the *Gita* and *Manusmruti* to the Ganges (38). Thus it could well be argued that the narrative rejects the notion of Sanskritization and suggests its counter movement of Dalitization as illustrated by Pavithran's silent and small acts in the Paraya slum.

> The era of symbols has not ended yet. The genitalia of time were still fertile. The seascape of saintly signs, departing and dying waves of the Ganges became the great pain of space and water. What have I thrown away? Opening the third eye of the subaltern, Krishnan Uncle said to Bhavathrathan, "*Manusmruti*!" (38)

In his flat in Hong Kong Chandran narrates the tales of his ancestors' confrontation with the caste question to his beloved Rosemary Wagner. Chandran describes *Manusmruti* as "the *Mien Kamph* of the Brahman" (38). But Rosemary aptly picks up the contradiction in this discourse: "I am pointing towards the contradiction in narrating the five thousand years of Indian cultural continuity and the lack of it at the same time" (38). And this is precisely the central contradiction and irony of the narrative itself and that of the cultural history of India. This unique blend of "culture" and barbarity is the core conflict of India abbreviated in the word "caste." It is also the underlying narrative element that is the cause of its vital creative tension. It also problematizes the narrative voice by making it double voiced, self-referential and auto telic. The central contradiction of caste is further developed here:

> The secrets of caste are embarrassing. Failing in the contest those castes who had fallen in to the down trodden status on one side; and on the other side caught

> up in a mysterious physics Parayas searching for the inner secrets of earth, the magical humans who resumed research in the asylum of untouchability and exclusion, those who could exchange bodies. The nuclear physicists of my ancient hamlet. (39)

Though untold it could be the same caste that could have lead Pavithran to the Paraya slums in Tholannur and made him enter in to their strange arts. He too indulges in the ancient and silent pursuit of his ancient brethren. Rationalist and communist Chamiarappan thus lost his hope in his elder son and he sends his brother Mayappan's son Gopalan to England for education. But even in the London pub where Marx enjoyed his beer and books he is haunted by the shadow that he thought he had shed away in his homeland. His girl friend Millie asks him about caste:

> One noon Millie accidentally asked about caste. In the cheerful spirit of the beer Gopalan became threatened. 'We could talk something else' he said. 'Did anything hurt you, something on untouchability and pollution?' she asked. The enigmatic threat of caste peeping into the pub of Karl Marx. Entering the pubs the violent youth attacked Jews and communists. But his personal pain took Gopalan's attention away. He was not bothered about all this. The light of the empire is everywhere; where ever you go you are second rated. Need to come out of this skin cover of the downtrodden. Could convert to Christianity, but it was not a solution. Though colonialism modernized its colonies it did not even touch Varnasrama and caste. Varna and Caste became the chief instruments of colonialism to govern the masses of India, as they became the topic of Millie's study. (42)

Contemporary historiography has already established this notorious compromise of colonialism with Brahmanism and patriarchy in India.[9] The so-called interventionist regimes and even missionaries collaborated and compromised to a great extent in retaining the old power structures and hegemonies, apart from tremendous educational and evangelical endeavours. That is the double labyrinth of caste and Christianity in India. Though Christianity has no caste, Christians have caste in India and in Southeast Asia. The narrativization of Caste Christianity in *The God of Small Things* would illustrate this point concerning the operation of caste hierarchy among Christians in Kerala, where Syrian Christians are equated with the Savarnas.[10] Though Islam has no caste, Indian Muslims too are caste sensitive. We also have bloody riots every year between upper caste Sikhs and Dalit Bahujan Sikhs. Gopalan's dilemma in the London pub therefore was not quite simple:

> In his apartment, alone, Gopalan thought of escaping the Hindu slavery. Christianity was of little help. Old uncle Chamiarappan's conversion to Christianity could not even touch caste. The strong bond between caste and the empire closed the doors of liberation. Being a subject of British India had only emphasized his subalternity. No more of this, one needs to inhale the air of equality and be free at last. (43)

He converted to Islam and became an ardent campaigner for the faith. He became Imtiaz Hassen. As an anti-British campaigner he got asylum in Germany. But his selfless love for his beloved Jessica Bloom, a Jewish woman, brings his life to an end in the endless torture of a Nazi concentration camp.

Another important aspect of the narrative is that though it is a long and fragmented narrative by Chandran as told to his beloved Rosemary in their Hong Kong apartment in the few hours before they lose themselves in the cyclone Angela, it has come to him through the stories narrated by several generations of grandmothers of the Ponmudi household. All this family lore as preserved and handed down from generation to generation orally through the intimate and affectionate narratives of grandmas also came to Chandran through his Devaki grandma. Actually he was born and brought up in it in the old Ponmudi ancestral home, and as a sensitive child he picked up and developed its core conflict of Caste that seemed unresolved. Thus generations of narratives and narrators and voices and perspectives converge in Chandran and his own voice seems lost in this polyphony.[11] It gives the novel a unique narrative structure but again the focal point is that of Caste and the Avarna struggles against it. The grandma narratives and the family lore converge in Chandran to be codified, edited and rendered in a standardized form that gathers and recreates the unwritten and often excluded Avarna domestic history.[12] It is also a textualization of the unwritten histories of the other in the medium of the fictional narrative, creatively erasing the boundaries of history and fiction, extending the peripheries of the narrative and margins of epistemologies.

This unique union is again exemplified in the frequent historical references to the practices of caste and untouchability. Discrimination in public spaces and places of worship like that of the Vaikom temple in central Kerala and the history of the struggle for temple entry and worship are also evoked:

> The disturbed generations of Ponmudi were not ready to retire and rest. They knocked at the doors of closed darkness where Krishnan Uncle had knocked before. Not for the nuances of Vedic chants but to ridicule the Gayatri mantras of concubines. The omnipresence of injustices caught their conscience. They blackened the 'Brahman only' boards of cheap railway restaurants. The passiveness of society was all pervasive accommodating these small protests. Over the sanctum sanctorum of Vaikathappan, Thotutaya Sivan, Chatayan, the ancient snake charmer, the Adi Dravidian trembled in wrath. His hand shook the towers and pillars of the temple and the untouchable devotees who were waiting outside for generations felt the tremor. (52)

Another reference is to the Avarna struggle for using public roads, for the basic freedom of movement. It is again connected to another historic struggle at Kalpathy in Palghat, reference to which was made at the beginning of this chapter.[13] The details of this might be relevant at this juncture.

> The Kalpathy road also belongs to the public roads in general that are built and maintained on public funds raised by taxing people like me. So I too want to walk on it, my Thalacheruman (chief Pulaya assistant) too..leading a group of educated Avarna youth Chamiarappan entered the Kalpathy road..he looked back and saw a mob in formation. He was unmoved. The rationalist and the divine dogma confronted each other. Chamiarappan felt bamboo rods falling on his back and the head being pierced as in fever. Nothing more [..] 'what Suppamani is he finished?' (in mixed Tamil and Malayalam) [..] languages can interbreed. It is denied only to the Human clans by the *Gita* and Manu. (59-60)

Marking Chamiarappan and his fellows with stones as if they are dead, the Brahmans retreat. Recovering from this long unconscious state Chamiarappan declares that he is no longer Chamiarappan, but Theodore. So all these historical references in the fictional narrative register and reinforce the construction of epistemological sites and resources about the Bahujan struggle in the making of Kerala and Indian society a democratic one that is overshadowed and erased in the celebrated nationalist historiography and the popular hegemonic notions about social transformation monopolized by the Savarna mainstream movements of Nationalism in India.[114] The grass root level democratization of the society was carried out through the formation of untouchable Avarna subjectivities and their mobilization into democratic groups called communities. Thus the democratization of Kerala is inseparably linked with the politics of the Avarna subjectivity and communitization.[115] This was a struggle against the internal colonization of caste in sharp contrast to the Savarna version of the nationalist movement, the breeding ground of imagined and chauvinist Hindutva revivalism that is taking fierce proportions into the formation of an Indian Fascism.[16]

This struggle to defy and escape caste is also connected and contrasted with the greater questions of race and ethnicity in the story of Gopalan, son of Chamiarappan's brother who becomes Imtiaz in Europe. He marries Jessica Bloom, a German Jew, and is exterminated as he prefers to share his beloved's destiny in her last days (61). Velappan, Chamiarappan's son-in-law also experiences caste-Swaraj within the British police force. He confesses to his wife that "the caste system in the service is more severe than outside" (264). Though he could not confront the internal caste system of the British service, he addresses the old ones:

> As an Avarna Velappan experienced a more extreme form of humiliation than the slavery of his motherland [..] in the teashop there are separate seats for Savarnas and Avarnas. Avarnas must wash the glasses clean after use...(95)

When he became Subedar Major in the M S P he revisits this tea-stall and hits back at the Savarna man who asks him to wash his glass. As he leaves the shop the crowd gives him way. Later he comments to Pankajakshy that it was the same crowd that lynched Chamiarappan in the Kalpathy street. The difference was only that there was the crown of the British emperor on his shoulders:

> 'Doesn't the country need freedom?' Asks Pankajam. 'whose country you mean?' 'I don't know. Father used to say that we should see greater truths forgetting minor disputes. He is in the Congress, does that harm us in some way?' [..] there was a force behind my hand that beat Chappan Nair and the crowd that gave me the way. The justice of the British emperor. The crown on my shoulder. (96)

The complexity of the problem puzzles Velappan as he arrests the nationalists from the Congress. The awareness of an internal colonization by caste and Brahmanic Hinduism as against British imperialism is a major concern in the novel. It is recognized by recent scholarship that, for the Bahujan masses of India the lasting empire was only that of caste and Brahmanic hegemony. The European colonial regime which ruled India for less than two hundred years and its politico-economic exploitations were only secondary to thousands of years of Brahmanic-Vedic-Hindu hegemony and colonization. The British-Raj and the colonial administration in a sense opened up the world for the subaltern. In 19th century western India the Shudra intellectual Phule welcomed the colonial rule, the missionary education, the colonial administration and judiciary. He appealed to his Satysodhak Samaj not to join the elite Brahmanic nationalist movement.[17]

At least from the Indus valley devastations to the present, Brahmanic internal imperialism is still continuing through its various avatars. The western intervention and the option of religious conversion opened up a revolutionary liberation discourse for the Bahujan thinkers like Mahatma Phule and Narayana Guru. Phule equated his Baliraj with that of the kingdom of Christ and Narayana Guru declared that it was the British who gave him the right to knowledge, as against the Ramraj where the Shudra ascetic Shambuka was beheaded by the lord himself.[18] Dr Ambedkar himself comes from an untouchable Mahar family that had the privilege of receiving English education for three successive generations. Mr. Ramji Sakpal, the father of the architect of Indian constitution, was an instructor in the British Army. The radical realization of the problematic of the internal imperialism of caste and Brahmanic Hinduism as against western imperialism and the urgent need to tackle the former is also articulated in the poetry of rationalist revolutionary poets like Sahodaran Ayyappan as well as that of Asan who is considered a somewhat Hinduized and

Sanskritized poet in Malayalam. Building upon the tradition of internal critique and the polyphony of subjectivities in the nationalist appraisals, *Thalamurakal* also registers the difference of experience and the individuality of Kerala's renaissance, which is in sharp contrast to its counterparts in the rest of the country, which were largely Hindu reformist attempts led by Arya and Brahmo Samajs, as in the Bengal renaissance. It is more appropriate to describe this as a cultural revolution that took place in Kerala in the late nineteenth and early twentieth centuries. It was the result of the struggles of the Avarna movements that experienced and identified this internal caste imperialism. The missionary interventions that brought to the forefront for the first time the question of social justice and human dignity had tremendous influence on some of these movements including the Narayana Guru movement that mobilized the Ezhavas in a process of democratic communitization. Other radical movements like the Sahodara movement and the Ayyankali movement effectively continued the democratic process that led to a radical reshaping of the social hierarchy. The Avarna experience of caste-empire at the heart of the nationalist discourse is what distinguishes Kerala's social transformation from other social renaissance movements in the rest of the country.

These greater questions concerning colonial intervention, internal imperialism and the homogenizing meta-narrative of nationalism are thus effectively narrativized in the subtle but meaningful ambiguities and intense dilemmas of Velappan the colonial servant who hesitates to arrest a nationalist Congress man in the novel (96-7).

Chamiarappan confronted this internal empire of caste with his rationalism, again signifying and textualizing another major ideology that struck the Avarnas, and Ezhavas in particular, at the beginning of the last century. This was articulated in the rationalist movement of Sahodaran K Ayyappan who re-interpreted his teacher Narayana Guru's message as 'No Caste, No Religion, No

God, but Dharma, Dharma and Dharma' with a neo-Buddhist ethical praxis, and initiated a series of inter caste dining and marriage practices in central Kerala.[19] Chamiarappan's conversion to Christianity was only a symbolic act of his exercise of will and his liberty of thought and belief (98). Soon after his entry into the fold he identifies caste in Christianity:

> There is caste discrimination in the Christian church, though the parsons do not preach it. They have their separate assets and estates. The Catholic Church of the southern 'elders' and the Basal Mission of the north Malabar both are trying to woo me into their folds. Even the Pentecoastal church that does not have much following does not spare me. Pastor Timothy is their man. Though they lack money they talk directly to God. A church without a parish. (147)

The choice of conversion gave the untouchable Bahujans at least a temporary way out of caste hegemony, though it constructed new hierarchies in more paradoxical reality formations within the promised spaces of Christianity, Islam and Sikhism. [20] In Travancore there were even conversions to Sikhism. It was a great act of defiance and a challenge to the Savarna hegemony as we locate these conversions in historical context. Though it gradually gave way to new elitist claims and monopoly claims, the environment created a radical turmoil in the social sphere that anticipated the above-mentioned cultural revolutions in Kerala. The narrative elaborates with the help of the striking image of a viper, caste retreating into the dark depths of the collective unconscious and lying dormant there:

> These conversions couldn't kill caste as such. Like a viper caste retreated in to the darkness of sleepy memories. pale skinned Christians traced their origin to the Brahman illams. According to Raghava Menon's account, if their forefathers were Brahmins then the carpenters,

> porters and toddy tappers of the highlands were also once Brahmans. Simple arithmetic! (150-51)

As mentioned earlier, the option of conversion gave a platform for collective bargaining to the untouchable Avarnas. And it also played a role in the events that led to the official proclamation of temple entry for the Avarnas in Travancore. The evangelical educational intervention too played a critical role in the social uplift of the Avarnas in Kerala:

> The temple entry proclamation of Travancore that weakened the Nivarthana Prakshobham,[21] influenced, though not directly, the baptisms of Palakkadu. Conversion only remained in Ponmudi and certain other elite households. Many had simply adopted names like Theodore. Seeking a social space to intervene, established churchmen from Travancore and Germany came to Ponmudi, seizing the opportunity. Only when the Christian priests came the people switched over to Christian attire and prayers. Having no other way some became paid pastors and preachers. (152)

In the story of Imtiaz and Jessica the caste question is connected to the greater questions of ethnicity, nationality and the terrors of the Nazi regime. The same notions of cultural and racial supremacy are seen operating behind the Aryan supremacy theory of the Fascists, providing parallels with that of Brahmanism. This is the lesson one learns from the story of Gopalan (later Imtiaz) who runs away from the caste-curse of his country, only to confront a greater curse, that is, of race:

> The Nazi soldier asks, 'Who is she?' Imtiaz said, 'Yes, she is my wife.' The Nazi spits on Gopalan's face. Imtiaz is shrieking under the whipping. 'You, who belongs to the vulgar castes, who defied the Aryans, do you have a wife? Say mate, the female one that multiplies the number of vulgar castes, or simply say whore, the Nazi roared [..] 'Which whore has given birth to you?' Gopalan didn't

reply. The question was repeated with the pain of whip falling on his face. The sergeant who was enjoying it from inside said, enough. Picking the collapsed man from the ground the soldier continued his torturous questioning. 'Who is the pig who impregnated your mother?' 'I was running away from India' realizing its futility, Gopalan said, 'from Caste.' The whip once again began its rise and fall. From another time and space Chamiarappan cried, 'No, no!' (241-42)

Decades later Gopalan's nephew and Chamiarappan's grandson Chandran writes about this story of the Ezhava Muslim who died in Nazi Germany for his Jewish woman, as he works on the caste conflicts of India for an international human rights publication (301). There are several junctures in the narrative where Chandran as a young man is presented as haunted by the memories of this trans-continental exile from caste that has proved futile. The implication of this is that the caste question is not just a question of memory, but is a contemporary political reality in the present of India. The signification is certainly that of the sustenance of hegemony.

From his childhood Pavithran, the elder son of Chamiarappan moved in the company of the Parayas of the village, who were considered further below the Ezhavas in the caste hierarchy. Though Chamiarappan could not understand this 'downward' move of his son, we see him taking a new turn towards the end of his life as he starts working among the scavengers of the suburbs of Palghat. This radical identification with the underprivileged castes is in sharp contrast to the desire for upward mobility in the Savarna social space and is reminiscent of the ethical praxis of 'Pulayan Ayyappan.' It is not a paternalistic or patronizing effort but is a democratic act, a process of Dalitization that is in sharp contrast with the failed attempt of Sanskritization enacted by Krishnan Uncle in Ponmudi.[22] Both upward and downward movements in social hierarchy are signified in the text as confrontations with the caste question. While Krishnan Uncle represents the upward mobility of Sanskritization and its futility, the downward movements of Pavithran to the Paraya slums and later of Chamiarappan to the Thotty (scavenger) slums represent the anticipated democratic process of Dalitization.

As a fictional narrative that represents the material context of caste Brahmanism in India, *Thalmurakal* anticipates the more democratic, decentered and humane process of social transformation that integrates the margins without patronizing pride into the democratic and egalitarian polity. The narrative stands puzzled in this dual dilemma in the irrational psyche of Pankajakshy:

> The memories of Ponmudi overflowed. From the sacred thread of Krishnan Uncle to Pavithran's occult arts of the Paraya ghetto. To where have Ponmudi voyaged? (319)

The role of the English language in subduing the reign of caste too is given voice, through the story of Stella Stanley, a Dalit convert to Christianity, who masters the master's language with a vengeance to overcome the Sanskrit epistemology and its world view.[23] She is the daughter of Chelly, the childhood companion who tells Chandran about 'the arrow of Rama,' and was in turn baptized by Chandran as Jesus Christ. As Chandran becomes a journalist she writes to him asking for support. She wants to write in all the leading journals about the caste imperialism of India. As Chandran concludes, like colonial justice and law-and-order administration, the English language also activated the speaking of the subaltern, by opening up a new vista and linguistic domain for the voiceless in India by de-legitimizing Sanskrit as the language of knowledge/power and also abolishing its meta-referential authority. Chandran writes to his parents:

> I took it as a joke when father said about the Malabar Special Police being a national movement. But I understand its meaning now. If there is any role for a

language in abolishing the caste system, it is English. Like M S P, English also becomes an instrument of our national movement. (340)

At this advanced stage in the narrative the multiplicities of voices seem to converge on the focal point of racial amalgam and organic human continuum as Chandran and Rosemary Wagner sacrifice themselves in the cyclone to bring into the world their hybrid child Theodore Vel Wagner (344). The name of this 'future' child is again significant in that it articulates a plurality of identities, a multiplicity of praxis and ideology and a polyphony of cultures and ethnicities. Theodore is the Christian name of Chamiarappan his grandfather bearing the marks of his rationalism and his defiance of caste. Vel is a common south Indian name invoking the old Dravidian god Velan or Murugan, a popular deity of the Bahujans from the Cankam period. And Wagner is his mother's surname connecting his umbilical cord to the blue blooded races of Europe. A movement from external political realities and socio economic formations to personal and individual reconciliation and transformation could also be identified in this evocative denouement.

Thus after taking up fundamental questions of caste, conversion, communitization and Dalitization, as well as that of the democratization of the polity and culture, the narrative retreats to the realm of domestic and individualistic reconciliation or a resurrection at the micro political or bio political level. This broad movement from the socio culturally political to the micro political could be identified in the whole gamut of Vijayan's writing, especially with reference to his historic critique of the Left and progressive politics in Kerala. It could again be contextualized and read in the subduing of radical ideology and the eroding of faith in collective struggles and movements in a maturing writer and representative subjectivity in the wake of the commoditization of the third world Left under corporate global capital. Again this attitude of the writer also poses questions on the effect of aging and illness on subjectivity, voice and agency of articulation. Yet the chunk of the argument and critique aims at the progressive mainstream discourses that evade the socio cultural and historic reality of caste and ethnic stratification of economy and polity in India, and the everyday material reality of multiplying and metamorphosing Brahmanic hegemony. If this is the case of historically marginalized backward communities, the conditions of the Adivasis who are generally imagined as outside the caste system is worse in the all pervasive purity-pollution discursive contexts.

One of the major trends in relation to the Adivasi or tribal debate in India has been that of de-contextualizing it from the discursive contexts of Varna, Caste and Brahmanism. Though it is done in a tactful and covert manner, the general assumption of these debates is the belief that Adivasis have always remained outside the caste system. The reference here is of course to eco-gurus like Ramachandra Guha.[24] What is of significance here is the epistemological function of such a discourse in the present. It erases the history of calamities that Brahmanism has imposed on indigenous and nomadic tribes throughout the peninsula. It erases the history of work and toil by the human productive forces of indigenous or ideologically subordinated tribes, that has gone into the making of Brahmanic caste villages and the legitimizing role of the Varna theory in the mobilizing of them in a process that sociologists define as 'from tribe to caste.' The emerging alliance of a Dalit Bahujan - Adivasi solidarity is cleverly forestalled by such interpretations. The absurdity of the eco-discourse is that not just the Adivasis, but the Dalits as well as Bahujans, who are grouped together as OBCs (with negligible regional exceptions, since in some states Shudras too are included) were also outside the caste system. The Bahujans were not ascribed any Varna status by Brahmanism and were called the Avarnas. But though they are outside, they are the basic working and productive communities that bear the brunt of the Brahmanic caste violence. There are also profounder praxis targets to this discourse. Foregrounding the "tribal" and silencing the Dalit Bahujan is the immediate outcome of this status quoist discourse that calculatedly subverts the democratic process of communitization.

This is the context in which the Malayalam novel *Mavelimantam* communicates itself to the reader. The novel narrates the struggle of the Adivasis under feudal lords for survival in Wayanadu in Kerala of the late nineteenth and early twentieth centuries.[25] Slave trade, colonial invasion, the Pazhassy revolt and other uprisings form the background of the narrative. The story revolves around the attempted escape to the forest of slave couples from bondage. It concludes with signs of anticipated liberation and hope.

The fundamental factor of relevance here is this hurried or abrupt closure of the narrative. The narrative ends even before the birth of the state (of Kerala) or of the nation, in spite of its passionate references to the valour of Pazhassy and Kunkan. This happens precisely because the two world wars follow this critical moment at the onset of the twentieth century and the great famine and depression in the country lead to the hurried migration of Syrian Christians from Travancore to Malabar, specifically to Wayanadu.[26] This migration has been a critical juncture in the history of the Adivasi land question. The migration pushed the Adivasis to the condition of landless slaves, further deteriorating their social and economic conditions. It also prevented their social mobility and communitization during the renaissance reforms that mobilized the other untouchable Bahujans and Dalits in the state in the early twentieth century. As the author of the narrative that deals with this precarious moment in history, K J Baby, himself a second generation Syrian Christian migrant, is under question for this abrupt ideological closure of his narrative. By covering the history of migration and land poaching through a skewed portrayal of feudal barbarism that happened in an earlier period by Menokis and Nambiars, Baby is playing hide and seek. Any reader of Kerala, having a vague sense of history would be amused at this hurried and abrupt conclusion of the novel, except for a few like K Sachidanandan who has contributed an introduction to the novel. Sachidanandan views the novel as a contribution to the "subaltern and ethno narrative" genre in Malayalam. For him it narrates a tale of resistance and of future struggles. The narrative with a retrogressive effect and a fragmented structure, something that reminds us of eighteenth century tribal oral narratives, then, is a site of fierce contestation.

The myth about Viratpurushan and the pseudo lords ("Kallathampurans") who subordinated the people's leader Maveli and his Mantam, the clan has been effectively utilized in the text to explicitly register the fact of Brahmanic Varna hegemony over the Adivasis. It is also important that Dalit Bahujan thinkers from Phule onwards have utilized and interpreted the myth of Bali for the people throughout India.[27] This liberation myth has been latent in their collective consciousness, which is articulated in the narrative through Jevaraperuman, an old slave. It is also interesting to read the subordination of the Adivasis not through force but through ideological factors like superstitious stories about other worlds, the under worlds of the darker gods. These Brahmanic deities haunt them in this world and the other. For them therefore there is no escape even in death. The battles of the other worlds and of the unconscious are fought by some of the daring ones in the tribe and they are in search of liberation, at a juncture where the very idea is unthinkable to their people.[28]

Thus the metaphysics of purity and pollution, of the construction, diffusion and control of fear, sin and guilt, the notion of hierarchy, and other ideological apparatuses of subordination were extensively used in the Varnadharma pattern by the upper castes (specifically mentioned as

Thampurans, Menokis and Nambiars in the narrative) in the construction of the Adivasi margin.[29] So both the caste question and the ideology of Brahmanism are central to the Adivasi issue and the narrative here. Actually Chapter One of the novel articulates the caste factor in the Adivasi reality through the reference to the Adivasis as "the lowest of all castes"(20).[30] It also equates them with darker beasts like buffaloes:

> For the Thampurans, slaves and buffaloes are the same. Like buffaloes the slaves must do the work they are asked to do. They are the same for them. (24)

The human is pushed down to the level of the beastly through associations established through the exercise of power. The psychological impact of this association is that the enslaved too begin to associate themselves with the beasts by convention. After all, they get only kicks and rotten food for the hard day's toil. Even eating rice is a "Thampuran privilege." The conditions in which they are kept without proper shelter and clothing too is degrading. They cannot even sleep like humans. Having no clothes to cover their bodies with, they herd together to survive on the heat of the other's body:

> Leave the question of sleeping, just had to lie straight. Even that is impossible. All lie like piled leaves, men and women, children and the old. (26)

In such dehumanizing conditions some of the younger ones ask old Jevaraperuman for his response to this injustice. The old slave observes: "With swords and words they degrade the human in us. To make mere beasts of us. Thampuran, is it so easy every time? You yourself become beasts for every beating that you inflict on us" (27). The story of Maveli Mantu and his Mantam of primitive equity becomes the most subversive weapon from Jevara's memory. As mentioned earlier, this myth of an egalitarian past and the intervention of the three "Kallathampurans" or pseudo-lords and their ideological cunning demonstrated in the fabrication of the story regarding the 108 Kulas and Jatis (28) are significant again in the context of the Varna ideology of Brahmanism. It is also interesting to note that this myth helps the thinking among them to subvert the hegemony and to defy it. But look at the power of discourse; they are made to believe that even in the other world after death they have to serve the Karatithampuran, literally "the bear lord" and his lady, thc Cheriyamma:

> After death we will all end up in the under world, there too we have this Karatitamburan and Cheriyamma. There too we have the slavery of the lords. In deep pits in the ground gruel is filled for us to lick up as for dogs. (28)

The chief Jevaraperuman narrates the details of that golden past and the history of betrayal in the folk tale:

> Once we too had a good time. A time when we were not slaves to anyone. That was the time of Maveli Mantu. He was our chief, but there were no slaves and lords. We cultivated and ate together as equals. There were no Atiyans and Paniyans, no Kurichiars and Kurumars. All humans enjoyed equality. No cheat and no evil. Then came the "Kallathampurans" or pseudo lords. They wore the false smile of humans. Maveli Mantu accepted them with a whole heart. But in return they grabbed his land and clan. When the chief questioned the cheats they knocked him down, and the blood of Maveli fell on the Mantam land. They assaulted his daughter and the clan. They chained the people in to cages and Kulas. 108 Jatis were established. To legitimize this classification they proclaimed this metaphysics: Listen you sons of dogs, this world belongs to a super man called Viratpurushan.[31] We came from the head and hands of the Viratpurushan. You came from underneath his feat, and so you are our slaves. So, slaves, from now on your duty is to obey what we say. The whole earth belongs to us. On your feet to increase our fields and to make the

hills orchards. But they didn't move. The lords raised swords, still nobody moved. Where swords and spears failed the lords introduced the goddess with blood oozing sword, Mali with her dangling tongue dripping blood. We became the slaves out of fear, not of this world, but of the under world. We became Paniyars and Atiyars who go to one hill after the other for the lords, to make orchards and fields for them. (28-9)

This myth explains the significant role that god and religion played in the Brahmanical conspiracy of subordinating the tribes and organizing them into slaves in a feudal set up. It also exposes the male conspiracy and the patriarchal core of the Varna ideology. It further illustrates the ideology of the totem and taboo, of sin and the sacred, of the otherworldly fears that have enslaved generations of people; effectively utilized by the hegemonic power groups that are still surviving as monopoly groups and preventing democratic formations in society.[32]

Along with the myth of Maveli the "Melorachan-and-Keeyorathi" myth of escape constitutes a dream of resistance for the tribe. Melorachan and Keeyorathi were the first man and woman to attempt an escape from the shackles of slavery (27). But greater calamities were awaiting them. As they were tortured to increase the production for Menoki Thampuran, they even cease to be humans and stop procreating. But the learned Menoki knows that he needs more and more slaves to widen his farmlands, and thus begins the most beastly episode in the clan's history - forced procreation to generate slave children. Menoki refers to this as "Chavittu," - literally "kicking" - an animal act. He issues orders to intensify the kicking during night hours (38). Even biological sexuality has been doctored and manipulated for the sustenance of hegemony:

Chemmi was ashamed to hear Menoki's question: don't you do the kicking at night as I ordered? Yesterday

> Thampuran asked him whether the Pánichis conceived or not, since they need more slaves and slave children. (38)

Thus sex was used not only for subordination, as a site for aggression and assertion of hegemony, but it was also used for the reproduction of the slave generations and to ensure the beastly existence of the enslaved, as in Brahmanism, that denied the human status to the Chandals or the Avarna Bahujans. The construction of the beastly within the human and its legitimation were the critical tropes in Varna hegemony.

This beastly subaltern realm has been constructed through generations of torture. Menoki forcing Kaippadan to bury another slave who dies of some disease is a typical instance:

> Menoki ordered to push down the body into a small pit, by hitting it down with the pickaxe. Kaippadan couldn't and he received a rain of blows that broke his back. At last with a roar he hit the body with the pick axe. The body broke down in to pieces. 'Stamp down it you dog, down it you dog,' shouted Menoki. Menoki was amused as Kaippadan obeyed him. (41)

Enslaving and taming are done with a great deal of effort. The conditions and experience of the female slaves were the worst. They were mere slave-producing wombs. They are not merely called dogs but are literally kept to produce the young slaves in to the world. The Thampuran controls not only their bodies but their emotions and hormones too. It is he who decides when they mate and how much litter they produce. He also uses them as sexual slaves by night. He howls at night for their instant service:

> It is Thampuran who is howling for us out of the anger that Cheriyamma had gone to sleep. He wants to get on us. But we shouldn't go. We have to give birth to Thampuran's children (42). They had seen the tears of mothers who had to give birth to increase the slave force

> of the Thampuran. They felt their heart beat who couldn't even cry aloud seeing their young ones feeding on their breasts being taken away to be sold in the slave market like mere animals...so they have decided not to give birth to children and bring them in to this Thampuran world. (42)

This extreme form of protest that one can think of, that of self denial of one's sexuality and the human urge for procreation, reminds us of the intensity of torture and dehumanizing oppression that was historically inflicted on the working communities in India by the parasitic Brahmanic upper castes. It again connects the Adivasi experience to the Dalit Bahujan experience at large by shockingly bringing in parallels from Dalit poems like "Blood Wave" by Daya Pawar, where a similar sacrifice of sex and procreation is suggested as a way out of comprehensive hegemony.[33] As the narrative has it, even rice is forbidden to the Adivasis and it is a special privilege of the lords:

> On seeing us Karatithampuran roared. When lords eat, slaves shouldn't be even seen in the vicinity, which is the law. Since our hunger will give them ulcers. (47)

Whether it is Pazhasy or the British whoever gains the upper hand, the true sufferers of history in Wayanadu have been the Adivasis. It is they who fight and die, who suffer and live as casualties, as victims of vengeful persecution that each battle is followed by:

> They cut their fingers off, hung them over fire, forced sons to molest mothers and did much much more... (51)

This history of fear and torture rules over their consciousness and their unconscious, and it haunts Kaippadan even in his attempted escape. Even when he is making love, the very mention of Menoki's name freezes him in to inaction:

> The moment he heard the name of Menoki, cold and darkness struck him down. 'sorry to ruin your sleep, woman' he told her [..]. (64)

But Menoki is only a mediating instrument, a torturing apparatus, a privileged pimp, a glorified agent of Brahmanism. According to Brahmanic sacred texts, the fourth Varna, the Shudra, must be a lifelong servant to the Brahman. Menoki too is a subservient slave to his high lords, Subarayar and Manippattar; and when they abuse and curse him, they keep him aloof at his "Shudrappad" distance. The Shudra distance refers to the permitted distance that is allowed for a Shudra while approaching a Brahman.[34] Again we see here a classical hierarchical structure from Brahman to the mediating Shudras to the untouchable Bahujans down to the Adivasis as the lowest victims of Brahmanic hegemony and caste hierarchy, again bringing in the core issue of caste in to the picture:

> Subarayar Thampuran who came in a palanquin looked at his field. It was expected to grow, and he was not quite contented. The hill was still not razed down. He called his clerk Manippattar; 'was it you who told me that it has been turned in to a field?' Bending his head he went straight to Menoki, kept him at the Shudra distance, and called him names. As soon as he turned his back Menoki began beating up the puzzled slaves. (69)

The high lords are always eager to retain and sustain the caste system and its vocabulary. They keep on reminding the Menoki that he is a Shudra, and even before it is uttered Menoki's body falls into a unique servile posture:

> 'Call that Shudra Menoki...' said Subarayar. On hearing this Menoki assumed his Shudra position and bent his head. (70)

Even the white lords are amazed by the "Savarna Buddhi" or caste cunning of the feudal lords, who use music to make the workers work faster, by playing over their sense of rhythm (71).

Whatever be the extent of torture and exploitation they would not run away since the punishments for run-away slaves are severe:

> Needles were pushed in to their nails, faces were mutilated with the sting of black scorpions. They were chained and left alone in burial grounds and yoked along with buffaloes to plough the ground. 'Don't you see you sons of slaves, if any one dare to go beyond our words, you will be finished, slaughtered' hearing this roaring of Karatithampuran the slave clans began to shiver out of terror. Their tears were burning. (78)

But when the company and the white lords came with unquestionable authority and material sophistication the Brahmanic Varna practitioners and their companions of "honour" also found some excuse to compromise with the new regime. Any examination of Kerala history will reveal that these companions of "honour" were always companions of "superior" hegemonic groups. They were the sole attendants and bodyguards of power and naked barbarism of might and manipulative metaphysics. Being the products of the large scale feudal militarization in the fifteenth and sixteenth centuries, the sheath-less sword was their sacred weapon in maintaining Brahmanic caste hegemony over the working communities and they pushed them further away from the public sphere and from educational, cultural and symbolic capital. The self-fashioned samurais of Kerala found nothing wrong in their shift in loyalty under colonialism. The eagerness with which they receive the white man, even taking care to entertain his horse by providing it a special "Pandal" for shelter, is one of the effective enactments of this opportunism that also ensures caste cleavage and spacing:

> The white lord who is coming to rule the land crossing seas and hills is our Maveli. An exclusive palace should be built for the white lord alone. It should be decorated with the choicest leaves and flowers from the forest. Another Pandal for his men. Beyond that one more Pandal for his horse with proper food. Further beyond

> separate Pandals for the Chettys and Nairs and Nambiars. Far beyond it all slaves can stand behind some tree trunk without polluting them. (86)

The hierarchical structure of castes was maintained with cruel force. A typical Menoki version is provided in Chapter Twelve, where he questions Jevaraperuman about the runaway slaves:

> The silence of Jevara was an extreme offence in the Thampuran world. Menoki used his bamboo pole to shower blows on the slave's back. The clan ran in to the forest seeing this outrage. 'You will be finished, finished' shouted Menoki. The old man standing there with out a tear drop angered the lord and he used his rod again and again till the old slave broke down in to the soil. The cries of the hiding clan became louder even without their knowledge on watching this. Menoki ran in to them raising his sword and they retreated further and further in to the woods..Menoki put his long spear in to the mouth of Jevara to know whether he is dead or alive. He pushed it so down the old man's throat till his hand began to move to stop this brutal act. That very moment Menoki gave a sudden blow with the bamboo pole and the hand was broken. Menoki crushed the broken hand under his feet and the cries of mothers and children once again came up from the bush. Ambu Thamburan orderd to put the broken hand to his mouth. Menoki was planning to do the same even before the order was issued and he did so. 'No one should give him water or food' Thampuran ordered, 'no one should even talk to him.' (100)

If the males are inflicted with brutal bodily mutilations, the females are tortured through their sexuality and the organic power of reproduction. A few of the thinking women slaves realize that the birth of a girl child is therefore a double curse in the Thampuran world since it is only an addition to the Thampuran herd, that is, she is destined to produce more and more slave children, especially girl children (123). Along with their body and sexuality, their pain and shame everything is under control and manipulation:

> I t is the lords who robe us, and it is the lords who unrobe us. What is there in a slave's body that the lords have not seen? (130)

The body of the slave is an object of the master's gaze. The master manipulates and exercises his power over the slave's body by concealing and revealing it, by mutilating and subordinating it. The lord covers and exposes it according to his hegemonic fancies and fetishisms. He plays hide and seek with it in the same way as Baby does metaphorically with his material. This also reminds us of the forced practice of uncovering the breasts before the feudal and caste lords to reiterate their hierarchical superiority and unquestionable hegemony forced on the Bahujans by the Brahmanic upper castes in Kerala even in the early twentieth century.[35] Toward the end the slaves manage to get out of this physical, psychological and cultural hegemony and develop a counter-hegemonic discourse. This discourse demystifies and subverts the subordination myths of the lords: "To chain our ancestors in the Thampuran cage they invented sprits and demons and sent them around us. The lords nourished them on the blood of cocks and on tender coconuts, to follow us down to hell. They have grown along with our generations, anchoring our fears. We can now use them against the lords" (164).

The ban on slave trade by the British soon follows and the Adivasis for the first time are granted minimum level of work conditions. In the words of Karian, a member of the clan, the new developments are promising:

> In the company work place we can raise our clothes above waist level. We can also lower it below the knee. Woolen clothes for cold nights, and more clothes to wear. The whites don't treat us as bulls and beasts like our

Thampurans. They are going to end the slave trade! From now on we cant be sold or bought, cant be exported across seas. (170)

Thus the picture the narrative presents at the end is a seemingly promising one for the slaves. But as mentioned earlier, their history does not end at this promising moment somewhere around the beginning of twentieth century. And the worst thing in the Adivasi history in Wayandu, the Syrian Christian migration from Travancore, takes place at this point of history. The narrative however opts to conclude, with out making even a slight mention of this important event, leaving all the related questions and uncertainties open. The silence is pregnant with tales of atrocities worse than what Menoki and Karatithampuran actually perpetuate in the narrative. The tales told are cruel, but the untold ones are definitely more cruel. What is foregrounded in the novel is not the tribal present but the past of the tribals, that too very cleverly chosen particular pasts to eliminate the threat of present turbulence and the democratic process of communitization and construction of brotherhood among the victims of Brahmanism. The abortion of radical solidarities should be carried out at any rate, and that is where the world/view of the novelist meets with that of the Thampuran. The non-Dalit, Savarna/Syrian subjecthood of the author is the villain of the piece here.[36] The tribalism discourse that the novel creates, just like the orientalism discourse of the western scholars that celebrates and writes/reiterates the past of the victim, thwarts attempts by emerging radical and broader ideological formations from the present to subvert hegemony, and serves the goals of the forces of status quo.

Notes

1. O V Vijayan, *Thalamurakal* (Kottayam: D C Books, 1998). No published translation in English is available.
2. The reference to the Kalpathy struggle is a fictional rendering of the historic event in early twentieth century

Palghat. For accounts of this struggle, see C. Kesavan, *Jeevitasamaram* (Kottayam: N B S, 1990) 182, and P. Kesavadev, *Ethirpu* (Thiruvananthapuram: Prabhat, 1999).

3. All the subsequent translated extracts from the text (Malayalam original) are mine from the D C B, Kottayam edition of 1998.

4. See M S S Pandian, "Church and Social Change in South Travancore," *Economic and Political Weekly* 25 (1990): 1767-68. Also Dick Kooiman, *Conversion and Social Equality in India: The London Missionary Society in South Travancore in the 19th Century* (NewDelhi: Manohar, 1989) and Gauri Viswanathan, *Outside the Fold: Conversion, Modernity and Belief* (NewDelhi: Oxford UP, 2001).

5. See I Ahmed, ed. *Caste and Social Stratification Among Muslims* (NewDelhi: Lal, 1978) and "A Different Jihad: Dalit Muslims' Challenge to Ashraf Hegemony," *Economic and Political Weekly* 38 (2003): 4886-91; for detailed accounts of Dalit Bahujan Muslims and their experience of inequlity from caste Muslims. For the same question in Christianity see Ajay Sekher in Note 110 below.

6. Sumit Sarkar, "The Fascism of Sangh Parivar," *Economic and Political Weekly* 28 (1993): 163-67. Also see Stany Pinto, "Communalization of Tribals in South Gujrat," *Economic and Political Weekly* 30 (1995): 2416-19.

7. See Gail Omvedt, *Dalit Visions: The Anti Caste Movements and the Construction of an Indian Identity* (Madras: Orient Longman, 1995).

8. B R Ambedkar, "Annihilation of Caste," *The Essential Writings of B R Ambedkar*, ed. Valerian Rodriguez (New Delhi: Oxford UP, 2002) 263; and *Castes in India: Speeches and Writing of Dr Babasaheb Ambedkar*, Vol. I (Bombay: Govt of Maharashtra, 1982). For a critical evaluation see Gopal Guru, "Understanding Ambedkar's Construction of National Movement," *Economic and Political Weekly* 33 (1998): 156-57.

9. Tanika Sarkar argues that the colonial rule and the church compromised considerably with the Hindu Brahmanic patriarchy and uppercaste norms in retaining hegemony. Arunoday Guha is concerned about the double

labyrinth of Christian Dalit hood that robs the victims of their constitutional rights. The futility of Re conversion is the thrust of the argument in Biswamoy Pati since caste, not religion is the key factor. See Tanika Sarkar, Arunoday Guha and Biswamoy Pati in the bibliography.

10. Ajay Sekher, "Older than the Church: Caste and Christianity in the *God of Small Things*," *Economic and Political Weekly* 38 (2003) 3445-49.
11. The concept of polyphony is developed from Bakhtin's notion of the dialogic nature of language and the heteroglossia. See David Lodge, *After Bakhtin: Essays in Fiction and Criticism* (London: Routledge, 1990).
12. For a detailed account on the 'Avarna Renaissance' in Kerala that ascribes agency to the untouchable Avarnas, see Puthupally Raghavan, *Viplavasmaranakal*-III (Kottayam: D C B, 1995) 10-11. Also see P Chandramohan, "Social and Political Protest in Travancore: A Study of the SNDP (1900-1938)," M Phil diss., Jawaharlal Nehru U, New Delhi, 1981 and M S Jayaprakash, "Sree Narayana Guru and Social Revolution in Kerala," *Meantime* Sept.(2003): 8-11. And also see Reghu. For details of Ezhava social mobility and communitization see Fiippo and Caroline Osellas, *Social Mobility in Kerala: Modernity and Idenity in Conflict* (London: Pluto, 2000). See Robin Jeffrey also in the bibliography.
13. For detailed accounts of these historical events see Kesavan, *Jeevitasamaram* and also Kesavadev, *Ethirpu.*
14. For the conceptual category of the Avarna Renaissance in Kerala see Puthupally Raghavan, where he identifies the movements and leaders of the Kerala renaissance emerging from the untouchable Avarna communities in the late nineteenth century. And for a critique of Savarna Brahmanic Nationalist renaissance in especially north India see J Reghu, "Kolonialisavum Jativimarsavum" *Madhyamam Weekly,* Nov. 28 (2003): 28-32.
15. J Reghu, "Understanding Community: Viswakarmas," *Economic and Political Weekly* 38 (2003): 5304 contextualizes the process of communitization and understands community as distinct from class and caste.

It also discusses the role of Ezhava communitization and other Avarna communitization processes in the modernization and democratization of Kerala as used by Narayana Guru in delegitimizing the meta-referential structure of Brahmanic, hierarchical Hinduism. Also see his "Adhunika Keralavum Samudayavatkaranavum".

16. Jotirmaya Sharma, *Hindutva: Exploring the Idea of Hindu Nationalism* (NewDelhi: Viking and Penguin, 2003) identifies four important ideologues of Hindutva; Dayananta Saraswati, Swami Vivekananda, Sri Aurobindo and V D Savarkar- all north Indian Brahmanic/Savarna mystic god men becoming powerful icons of religious regeneration. Also see the review article by K N Panikkar, "Protohistory of Hindutva" in *The Hindu*, 2 Mar. (2004): 13.
17. Jotiba Phule, *Samagra Vangmay* (Bombay: Govt. of Maharashtra, 1990).
18. Gopal Guru, "Liberating Jotiba Phule," *Economic and Political Weekly* 38 (2003): 35 defends and contextualizes Phule's reading of colonialism from the Dalit Bahujan perspective and says it is possible to give multiple readings for colonialism. The historically marginalized sections who were made to suffer from cumulative disadvantages would be skeptical of the 'nationalist promise' and at times be supportive of imperial attempts that were making some space for these sections. Phule, Periyar and Ambedkar recognized the opportunities provided by colonial modernity. It is in this sense that one can understand Phule's attempt to compare Baliraja with Jesus Christ. Also see Sahodaran Ayyappan's interview with Narayana Guru, where he welcomes the western intervention. See Ayyappan, K. For a detailed analysis of colonialism and the emergence of nationalism in India see Partha Chatterjee, *Nationalist Thought and the Colonial World: A Derivative Discourse?* (Delhi: Oxford UP, 1986).
19. K A Subramanyam, *Sahodaran Ayyappan* (Kochi: K A Subramanyam and Kerala Sahitya Akademi, 1976); M K Sanu, *Sahodaran K Ayyappan* (Kottayam: D C B, 1986). Also see Raghavan and Kesavadev for somewhat impressionistic images of Sahodaran Ayyappan.

20. Rowena Robinson and Sathianandan Clarke, eds., *Religious Conversion in India: Modes, Motivations and Meanings* (NewDelhi: Oxford UP, 2003) specifically deals with conversion to religions like Sikhism, Islam and Christianity.
21. A collective political movement by Ezhavas, Muslims and Christians in early twentieth centrury Kerala for proportionate share in public service and education according to population.
22. Rudolf C Heredia, "Subaltern Alternatives on Caste, Class and Ethnicity," *Contributions to Indian Sociology* 34. 1 (2000): 37-62, takes up in detail the notions of Dalitization and Mandalization and anticipates a subaltern hermeneutics that could democratize society and polity.
23. S Anand, "Sanskrit, English and Dalits," *Economic and Political Weekly* 34 (1999): 2053-56 elaborates the hegemonic purposes of language and pedagogy in India.
24. See Ramachandra Guha, *An Ecological History of India* (NewDelhi: Oxford UP, 2002 (1992)) in which he legitimizes the Brahmanic Varna theory and the caste system "as a form of ecological adaptation" (109) in the guise of giving an ecological interpretation of caste. Also note his propagandist praise for Brahmanic Hinduism as "inclusive" (110). Also see his "Savaging the Civilized: Verrier Elwin and the Tribal Question in Late Colonial India," *Economic and Political Weekly* 31 (1996): 2375-89. On the other hand the notion of Adivasis as a greater community comprising various indigenous and nomadic tribal groups of people is developed and dealt with here as an evolving category through and in contemporary and historical writings and epistemological research encompassing various disciplines. See Verginius Xaxa, "Tribes as Indegenous People of India," *Economic and Political Weekly* 34 (1999): 3589-95 that articulates the internalization of the Adivasi category by the tribes as a mark of social differentiation, identity assertion and empowerment. See R V Bhuskute, "Tribals, Dalits and Government Land," *Economic and Political Weekly* 24 (1989): 2355-61 for the land grabbing disputes in post colonial India. For the details of the Hinduization of Adivasis see Stany Pinto, "Communalisation of Tribals

in South Gujrat," *Economic and Political Weekly* 30 (1995): 2416-19 that explores how Hindutva forces effectively converted the hitherto non-communal tribals of Gujarat in to Muslim baiters, the culmination of which was explicit in the Gujarat pogrom in 2002. Also see Rudolf C Heredia, "Tribal History: Living Word or Dead Letter?," *Economic and Political Weekly* 35 (2000):1522-25 that focuses on the hijacking of tribal history by nationalist or Brahmanic scholarship and the suppression of oral histories. The present analysis draws on these pluralistic and developing epistemological debates regarding the Adivasi question in India, which are departures from the monolithic reductionism of the earlier accounts that serve hegemonic purposes.

25. Dilip Menon, *Caste, Nationalism and Communism in South Inida* (Cambridge: Cambridge UP, 1994) 13-14, observes, while commenting on the relations between agrarian economy and the Nayar households of the early twentieth century in the neighbouring taluks of Wayanadu like North Kottayam and Kurumbranadu, that many large tharavadus (Nayar land lord households) built up informal empires by subordinating the tribal labour in the forests and through judicious alliances with other powerful tharavadus.

26. See K Ajitha, *Ormakkurippukal* (Kottayam: N B S, 1994 (1982)) 70, for a detailed account of the migration by Syrian Christians to Wayanadu and the subsequent incidents of land poaching by them and the alienation of tribals from their ancestral lands. Specifically see chapter six that deals with the migration to Pulpally, pages 49, 69 and 70. Also see C K Janu, *Mother Forest: The Unfinished Story of C K Janu, As told to and Written by Bhaskaran*, trans. Ravi Shankar (New Delhi: Women Unlimited and Kali for women, 2004).

27. For Phule's version of the Bali myth see Gail Omvedt's brief account in "Hinduism as Brahman Exploitation: Jotiba Phule" in *Dalit Visions: The Anti-caste Movement and the Construction of an Indian Identity* (New Delhi: Orient Longman, 1995). Also see Rosalind O'Hanlon, *Caste, Conflict and Ideology: Mahatma Jotiba Phule and*

Low Caste Social Protest in Nineteenth century Western India (Cambridge: Cambridge UP, 1988). For Phule's radical reading of the colonial intervention from the Bahujan perspective and his attempt to compare the praxis contexts of Bali and Christ, see Gopal Guru, "Liberating Jotiba Phule," *Economic and Political Weekly* 38 (2003): 3703-04.

28. K K Baburaj, "Mantakanavukalile Michasidhantham," *Mathrubhumi Weekly,* May 9 (2004): 18-23, reads this decomposed narrative craft as part of the decayed pattern obtaining in Malyalam modernism that denied human status to the subaltern, a narrative that negates the possibility of Adivasi sustenance and struggle, but something that covertly imagines genocide.

29. For a detailed historical account of this Brahmanic social engineering carried out through their chief agents, the mediating Shudras, also called "companions of honour," see K N Ganesh, *Keralthinte Innalekal* (Thiruvanantapuram: Dept. of Culture, Govt. of Kerala, 1990), specifically the chapter on "Caste and Class" and the sections dealing with the transformation from the tribal to the feudal. Also see K K Kochu, "Swathutamastatayute Avirbhavam" (The origin of land ownership), *Madhyamam Weekly* Aug 31 (2002): 23-27, for a discussion on the formation of elite land holding groups in the Cankam period and the late enslavement of the tribal clans, who were ideologically subordinated and brought to bonded slavery.

30. All subsequent translations from the text are mine from the Malayalam original of K J Baby, *Mavelimantam* (Thrissur: Current, 2000).

31. Note that he is exclusively a Man not a woman, exposing the patriarchal core of the Brahmanic Varna ideology articulated through texts like *Gita* and *Manudharmasastra* or Smrities in general.

32. For the details of this contemporary hegemony see Andre Beteille, *Equality and Universality: Essays in Social and Political Theory* (NewDelhi: Oxford UP, 2002) where issues of caste hegemony in contemporary Indian society are analyzed in depth. For a comprehensive view of this growing inequality and the factors that sustain it see, K L Sharma, ed., *Social Inequality in India: Profiles of*

Caste, Class and Social Mobility (NewDelhi: Rawat, 2001). For an interesting account of the Varna – capitalism nexus in India see Franco F., "Ideology as Social Practice: The Function of Varna," *Economic and Political Weekly* 24 (1989): 2601-12. To see how the new economic policies and privatization drives are contributing to this historic inequality and marginalization see P G Jogdand, ed., *New Economic Policy and Dalits* (New Delhi: Rawat, 2000), specifically the chapters, " New Economic Policy and Tribal Reality", "Liberalization and the Tribal Problematique", "Impact of Development in Tribal Development in India" and "New Economic Policy and Tribal Development". For a continuous and analytical history of the caste hegemony and related power groups from medieval to the present time see Susan Bayly, *Caste, Society and Politics in India from the Eighteenth Century to the Modern Age* (Cambridge, Cambridge UP, 1999).

33. See Arjun Dangle, ed., *Poisoned Bread* and *Homeless in my Land* (Hyderabad: Orient Longman, 1999).

34. For details of Brahmanic spatial strategies and hierarchical spacing gradations in Kerala see P K Balakrishnan, *Jativyavastitiyum Kerala Charithravum* (Kottayam: SPCS, 1986) and also K N Ganesh and Robin Jeffrey.

35. See P K Balakrishnan. See P S Velayudhan, *S N D P Yogacharitram* (Kollam: S N D P Y, 1978) specifically the chapter on 'Nair-Ezhava riots' on page 147.

36. For the details of these categories and problematic subject positions see Ajay Sekher, "Older Than the Church: Caste and Christianity in the God of Small Things," *Economic and Political Weekly* 38 (2003): 3445-49.

5

Nation Versus Conversion : *Kanthapura, God of Small Things*

> He is mixing with the Pariahs as a veritable Mohammedan, and the Swami has sent word through Bhatta to say that the whole of Kanthapura will be excommunicated [...] he can go sleep with these Pariah whores[...] but let him not call himself a Brahman.
>
> (*Kanthapura* 57-58)

> They had jumped from the frying pan into the fire. They were made to have separate churches, with separate services and separate priests. As a special favor they were even given their own separate pariah Bishop [..] it was a little like having to sweep away your footprints without a broom. Or worse, not being *allowed* to leave footprints at all.
>
> (*God of Small Things* 74)

The blurb of *Kanthapura* proudly presents itself as a fictional rendering of the struggle for independence and of the way "the movement became a tangible reality in rural India."[1] This in itself could easily be identified as a homogenizing nationalist project, carrying the hidden agenda of the nationalist power elite of the Hindi – Hindu – Hindustani – Delhi type, described as "Hinduism/ Brahmanism as Delhi rule" by Gail Omvedt.[2] The meta-narrative of nationalism, the freedom struggle led by the Congress party and its caste Hindu leadership, specifically its Brahmanic heads, have always been puzzled by the pluralistic and multilateral nature of the subaltern, peasant and low caste movements that problematized the so called monolithic, anti-colonial liberation struggle of India.[3] It was also as an outcome of the political expediency of the hegemonic lords soon after independence to legitimize, narrativize, textualize, disseminate and manufacture consent and pedagogic consensus among the rural masses that nationalism and anti-colonial solidarity emerged as the only "true, patriotic and ethical" ideology and praxis. The nationalist elite also wanted to assert that patriotic cultural nationalism is the legacy of the martyrs and the republic; and those who questioned nationalism and its homogeneous discourse could only be termed as traitors of the motherland. In this hegemonic perspective the people who experienced the most degrading slavery in human history for thousands of years under the internal imperialism of Hindu/Brahmanic colonialism, and their liberation movements under the leadership of thinkers like Phule, Narayana Guru and Periyor become anti-nationalist and communitarian.[4] This is the discursive context in which nationalist narrative texts like *Kanthapura*, that attained instant canonical stature as a Gandhian novel and as the first artful appropriation of the English language by an "Indian" writer become significant.[5]

The nationalist project of using the creative imagination to engender a national psyche and liberal subjecthood is signified by the iconic status of Gandhi.[6] The Gandhian ideology and its peculiar way of evading the caste question through its patronizing double speak of *Harijanodharana* has been exposed in Gandhi's own time by the historic critique of Ambedkar.[7] The Gandhian ideology wants to resolve the issue of caste and hierarchy but at the same time it wants to retain the upper hand and agency for the Savarna population, who are expected to redeem the "Harijans." That is why Dalit Bahujans rejected it as paternalistic, elitist and non-egalitarian. *Kanthapura* articulates these concerns as well as the struggles and strifes of the split nationalist worldview that is complex in many ways.

It is the story of young Moorthy, an educated and idealist Gandhian Brahman of Kanthapura, a small hilly hamlet in the Western Ghats, and his attempts to disseminate the ideology of Gandhian Swaraj in the caste-ridden conservative Brahmanic society.[8] It is the typical enactment of the *Harijanodharana* project of Gandhian *Gramswaraj*.[9] The split psyche and the contradicting subject position of the nationalist Brahmanic elite engaged in this great redeeming task are explicit not just in the plot, but at the level of the narrative structure and voice. While the "great act of self sacrifice," of discarding the age-old Brahmanic elitist legacy of purity and pollution, is personified in the character of Moorthy, young, rebellious and forward looking, the textualization and narration of this complicit and precarious social transformation is recorded and rendered through the "mature" voice of an old Brahmanic female subject who lends the weight of hegemonic and hierarchical worldview to the process. Young Moorthy becomes the spirit of masculine reformism and the old feminine narrative voice stands for the domesticated hegemonic tradition and its hierarchical goals. The conflict between the young, radical and subversive, and the old, complicit and hegemonic is explicit in this central problematic of the narrative text.

Another narrative trope that articulates this tension is that of the old rural naïve communes, the prototype of *Gramswaraj*, the autonomous and self-sufficient village neighborhoods demarcated with occupational caste tags. The narrative deliberately develops a discourse of rural naiveté to whitewash and subdue the material conflicts and the inhuman suppression of caste and gender issues from within the boundary of this Brahmanic caste-swaraj village. This is a discourse of "ruralism" comparable to the discourses of "primitivism" and "orientalism" that too served the purposes of power and hegemony through material conquests and holocausts. This ruralism discourse should again be contextualized and epistemologically elaborated by placing it in the environment of the Gandhian ideology of Brahmanic patriarchy perpetrated in the name of *Gramswaraj* and *Harijanodharana*. The ruralism discourse also provides parallels with the tribalism discourse identifiable in the texts dealing with the Adivasi question like *Mavelimantam* (see the fourth chapter).

In the foreword to the novel, Rao himself asserts that "there is *no* village in India, however *mean*, that has not a Sthalapurana, or legendary history of its own." See the homogenizing and authoritarian voice with which he sums up the plurality of India, which could only be termed as Brahmanic/hegemonic. He himself relates and places his project in the tradition of myth-making that allowed Brahmanism to imagine and name the subcontinent and its territories, and thus played a key role in establishing its narrative monopoly over the Bahujan masses over thousands of years (see the discussion of "Parasuram Padalli," the village of *Gramayana* in the third Chapter). These hegemonic myths associate each and every bit of land to a Brahmanic saint or a subservient Kshatriya ruler like Rama who would ensure the supremacy and protection of the Brahman and the cow, thereby establishing a twice-born monopoly over the land and the material culture. By invoking the name of Rama, the legendary Aryan god who destroyed the Southern civilizations through cheat and opportunistic alliances and ensured the perpetuation and sustenance of Aryan–Brahman hegemony throughout the peninsula, and linking it with each and every village of the newly imagined nation, and also bringing in and associating the name of the Mahatma to it, Rao makes his message explicit. But one might ask what, or who gives him the authority and agency to speak for the people in an all-encompassing way invoking an Aryan ruler, and what is the legitimacy of his sovereign subject position as "we" and "ours."

Raja Rao also effects another important erasure and transcendence here. "We are all instinctively bilingual," he adds in the foreword. In order to defend his choice of the English language and his self-assumed spokesman-ship, he simply mocks at people who were always outside the power play of hegemonic colonial languages, whether it is Sanskrit or English, which were never spoken by the people at any given time. By invoking the legacy of *The Ramayana* and *The Mahabharata* and his own hybrid tongue of sophistication he also foregrounds these two hegemonic languages and the cultures that they represent. The "we" discourse that implies that the people of India are historically equal and are the homogeneous heirs to the hegemonic meta-narratives of the epics and the elitist canon again places the author at the centre of the nationalist project.

In the narrative "we" assumes voice in a mediated and patronizing way. It is the nationalist tastes and standards that are the ideals of the village conscience, and it is expressed through the discourse of "we" that voices the concerns of the Brahmanic value system. The monopolizing and policing collective consciousness informs and signifies its scopes and limits, the omnipresent and potent nationalist voice closely doctoring it:

> We never liked him (Dore). He had always been such a braggart. He was not like corner house Moorthy, who had gone through life like *a noble cow, quiet, generous, serene, deferent and Brahmanic, a very prince, I tell you*. We loved him, of course as you will see, and if only I had not been a daughterless widow, I should have offered him a grand daughter, if I had one. And I know he would have said: 'Achakka, you are of the Vedasastra Pravina Krishna Sastri's family, and is it greater for you to ask something of me, or me to answer 'yea." (12)

Thus Rao's text confirms that Brahmanism is an ideology, serene and deferent, a princely one, unlike the un-

Brahmanic or anti-Brahmanic ideology of the likes of Dore, perhaps an abominable individual like Naranappa in *Samskara*. Being princely Brahmanic therefore matters, since power matters.

Even in the spatial narrativization of the village one could see the Chathurvarnya structure that begins from the Brahman head and ends in the Shudra limbs. The caste-swaraj village is presented as an archetypal Utopia by the old feminine narrative voice. The Brahman quarter is mentioned and held at the top of the things in relation to space and social topography. The gradation and demarcation of material space and social life is narrated as something normal and eternal. The narrative chokes in repeated references in a secondary way to the Pariah quarter and the other untouchable quarters, which are the sole working quarters of this evil organism called the caste-swaraj village. Thus Brahman occupies the centre of space and time and the centre of reference of all the sign systems here. That is why the narrative voice is not even sure about the existence of the Pariah quarter with its countless huts (12), since the margins no longer exist in its cosmology and epistemology, it is an erased and constantly cursed presence, an imagined mirage.

Even the folk songs and popular entertainment of the Harikatha kind connect the freedom struggle with the Sanskrit meta-narratives of Aryan gods and goddesses, from the epics and Puranas, thereby ensuring the perpetuation of hegemony. They become elitist propaganda in disguise, a consent-manufacturing masquerade that proves to be of influence among the illiterate masses, among the Bahujans and women in particular. See the cross-reference and inter-textual invocations in the Harikatha:

> 'Today' he says 'it will be the story of Siva and Parvati.' And Parvati in penance becomes the country and Siva becomes heaven knows what! Siva is the three eyed, he says and 'Swaraj too is three eyed: self purification,

> Hindu-Muslim unity, Khaddar. And then he talks of Damayanti and Sakuntala and Yasoda and everywhere there is something about our country and something about Swaraj. Never had we heard Harikatha like this, and he can sing too, can Jayaramachar. He can rapt us in tears for hours together. But the Harikatha he did which I can never forget in this life and in all lives to come is about the birth of Gandhiji [..] the old woman came along [..] she could never stay away from a Harikatha. And sitting beside us, how she wept! (20)

Note how the hagiographies of the ancient and contemporary Brahmanic deities intercross and mutually contribute to the perpetuation of hegemony. The mythical and discursive contexts and paradigms from which the makers of neo nationalism draw their metaphors are revealed here. Damayanti and Sakuntala are typical feminine constructs who are subservient to Brahmanic patriarchy. That is why they are idealized cult figures in the modern Brahmanic imagiNation. The image of such "noble" women runs deep in the sacred symbology of the nation, which is to be protected from the invading and alien threats of the other. The vampires of patriotism and nationalism feed on the carcasses of these gendered subjects whose mind and body the masters literally govern.[9] By invoking and intertextually signifying the model women, model gods and godly men from the present, Brahmanic patriarchy inscribes its name over the new imagiNation. It is a way of monopolizing and appropriating the new nation, its past, present and future, that must be imagined and textualized. It is to be materialized through the mobilization of the Bahujan masses, without whose support the high priests of purity would remain lifelong servants to their 'flesh eating' white lords.

Even the might and administrative power of the colonial white regime could not penetrate the heart of Brahmanic darkness covering the sanctum sanctorum of caste-swaraj villages, since thecolonial regime did not want to disturb the society's power equations. The police inspector Bade Khan could not find a place within the Kantapura village since he is a Muslim and therefore a "mlecha" in the Brahmanic view. He settles outside the margins in an estate hut, but does not forget to ensure the custody of a poor Pariah woman as a sex slave. Both in the centre and in the periphery the gendered subject, especially the subaltern one, is at the receiving end. According to the narrative, the inspector is always eager to give the woman a "warmful bed" (27).

If these are aspects of cultural monopoly, in Bhatta, the village moneylender we have a typical embodiment of the aspects of economic monopoly. Bhatta is a slice of the Brahmin-Baniya money lending legacy that ensured economic development and monopoly for the noble lords who detested manual labor and material work as the Top Twice Born.[10] "Bhatta became richer and richer. He could lend out more money. And now he was no more a pontifical Brahmin. He was a land-owner...pariahs and plantation coolies were at the door" (38). Yet the narrative voice holds him in high esteem in comparison to the Chetties, the real tradesmen and therefore the real Vaisyas in the Brahmanic Varna system. In the hierarchical worldview of the female voice belonging to the gendered Brahmanical subject, they could be nothing more than the Padajas, or the most detested Shudras; "He (Bhatta) was so smiling and so good. Never had he charged us more interest than Subba Chetty or Rama Chetty. These two brothers were the ruin of our village (40)." Thus the curse is not for the acts and deeds but for the caste, since both persons do the same work. The pro-Brahmanic caste position and imagined subservient purity of Bhatta as a Vaisya with 'a second metaphysical birth and a sacred thread' is again stressed and projected in the general public (here Brahmanic) opinion of the village elders, who condemn his uplifting attempts of the Pariahs in the name of nationalism. Even the Brahmanical saints and high priests, canonized as Sankaracharyas and Swamis and as supreme spokesmen of Hinduism, want this subaltern uprising to be crushed in its seed:

> 'The Swami is worried over *this Pariah movement and he wants to crush it in its seed, before its cactus roots have spread far and wide*. You are a Bhatta and your voice is not a sparrow voice in your village, and you should speak to your people and organize a Brahman party. Otherwise Brahmanism is as good as kitchen ashes. The Mahatma is a good man and a simple man. But he is making too much of these carcass eating Pariahs. Today it is the Pariahs, tomorrow it will be the Mohammedans, and the day after the Europeans [..] we must stop this. The Swami says he will outcaste every Brahmin who has touched a Pariah. That is the right way to begin. Bhattare, we need your help.' (44-5)

So they want to keep the nationalist discourse and its greater legacy as an exclusive Brahman-Bania/Top Twice born/Savarna affair. From the beginning itself Brahmanic patriarchy is aware of the threat of the Dalit Bahujan appraisal and want to abort it in the womb itself, as female foetuses are aborted by patriarchy in contemporary India. The Brahmanic image of the Muslims and the Europeans along with that of Dalits and Bahujans as carcass-eaters and degraded aliens is also to be taken note of here. What is under threat in confronting all these others is always caste and the Varna Dharma metaphysics surrounding it, for the Swami says, "he will *outcaste* every Brahman who has *touched* a Pariah." And they are also sure that "this Bhatta who is a pontifical Brahman cannot be on the side of the Pariahs" (45). The second Brahman also rises to the occasion as expected by his earthly lords, the real first ones, and asserts; "I see no fault in Khadi and all that. But it is this Pariah business that has been heavy on my soul.." (46).

Though they could tame the rural Bhatta who is just a pontifical, would-be Brahman, they are not that sure about Moorthy and his city talk. They fear English and Western education. But one good old lady assures them: "Moorthy was such a deep-voiced, God loving person, and would do no mixing of castes" (51). See the masculine and caste-centred ideology of Brahmanic patriarchy speaking through one of its aged female subjects, for her Moorthy's deep-voiced manhood and expected/desired exclusivist assertion of caste hierarchy are promising. At least for her he is not an enemy of the age old power structure and a usurper of hegemony. But soon they find out that he is an enemy of the system: "he is mixing with the Pariahs as a veritable Mohammedan, and the Swami has sent word through Bhatta to say that the whole of Kanthapura will be excommunicated...he can go sleep with these Pariah whores...but let him not call himself a Brahman" (57-8). Again note the evil image and curse connected to the Muslims. In Brahmanical imagination that is the most degraded of states, without caste, hierarchy and 'culture.' It is a constant threat of pollution and otherness. The other is a constant threat of subversion and the loss of hegemony.

In receiving curses only the Pariah could surpass the Muslim. Not just the name of the low caste, even their shadow is polluting. In the *God of Small Things*, we have a reference to Dalits as dark shadowy creatures, not recognized as human beings and who are not allowed to leave their footmarks or shadows behind. They are violently denied their historical shares and basic human rights and assets. See how cunningly Indian Brahmanic nationalism tries to get rid of their shadows, even from the discourse of the domestic register. When Moorthy returns home after his *Harijanodharana* work, 'a great act of selfless redeeming' and patronizing, his mother welcomes him with this age-old curse, and threatens him on caste lines: "Don't talk like an innocent. Go and stand on the steps like a Pariah. Let not your shadow fall on me - enough of it" (62). The Pariah can even pollute the Brahman household and food through mere talking, via air: "Can't you shut your mouth, you Pariah!

... You always want to pollute the food of Brahmins with your evil tongues" (85).

Even when the honour of women is in question, caste honour sanctifies and legitimizes violence done on that ground and gains priority. The Brahman clerk's declaration defending his daughter from the Sahib is that "I am a Brahman, I would rather die than sell my daughter" (83). The narrative generously adds that after this the master hesitated to force even low caste women: "And when a Pariah says no, he hardly sends the Maistri to drag her up at night" (83). Thus the reader may conclude that the honour of women too is hierarchized according to the sacred Brahmanical Varna Dharma and that chastity and purity are more or less Brahmanic privileges and monopolies. The slave woman could not even imagine an autonomous human individual subject position. It was 'so natural and normal' that she could be dragged out of her ghetto and raped at the caste lord's convenience.

But the hard and fast rules of purity and pollution also change on certain occasions, especially when there is an urgent need for human power and resources. The ex-feudal Brahmanic caste lords otherwise keen on erasing the subaltern imprints of history have no problem in mobilizing the muzzle power of the untouchable Pariahs when it suits their interests. The untouchable masses form the backbone of all nationalist struggles and campaigns. The subaltern is cheated by the brief spell of egalitarianism and camaraderie, and they break their backs and limbs to defend the lords and their nationalist cause. Such opportunistic tactics are employed by the Savarna/Brahmanic leadership of all major political parties in India. Unfortunately, as illustrated by the *God of Small Things* and as economists like Amartya Sen have pointed out, the Left still maintains its historic avoidance of the caste question in its analysis of the Indian society.[11] And even after the collapse of the rhetoric of "the class struggle" in contemporary post-Mandal politics they have subverted the constitutional protection to the Bahujan backward communities by diluting the social justice foundation of affirmative action with their veiled neo rightist "economic justice" metaphysics. Reservations were never constitutionally intended for economic uplift or levelling but for social and educational backwardness. Social justice was its primary concern, not economic uplift. So we see the Left working in tandem with the Savarna upper caste organizations and asking the democratically elected government in Kerala not to implement the social justice policies and constitutional liabilities in the wake of the debate initiated by the Narendran Commission Report that came up for discussion in 2005, on the question of recruitment to the public service. The erasure of historical inequalities, characteristic of the ex-caste lords in the nationalist elitist tradition articulated here should also be seen in this hegemonic contexts and general pattern of diplomatic policy shifts, that have engineered society and its economy.

So it is the Pariahs who receive the blows here and also it is their quarter of the village that gets destroyed in the agitations (121). Towards the end of the struggle they are getting out of the picture altogether (122-3). It is significant that the Brahman quarter stood untouched by the violence and calamity of the nationalist struggle. The colonial police men consisting mainly of caste Hindus use the upsurge to reiterate caste hegemony by using violence on the Pariah women, who are raped brutally on caste lines, anticipating the final solutions in Gujarat:[12] "The yell of the Pariah women still comes rolling across [...] a police man upon her [..] from the Pariah street we hear nothing but shouts and lamentations [...] the shrieks of Pariah women are still shrill in the air"(213). The participation and mobilization of women in the nationalist movement is a problematic issue in the light of new insights on gender violence and related cultural questions. It is a lot more complex issue than the mobilization of their men, whose work force and labour resources are cheaply exploited by the Brahmanic upper caste leadership.

Moorthy who is presented as a selfless Gandhian and a representative of the nationalist Brahmanic elite, asks the fellow nationalists to put aside the purity and pollution of caste for awhile till the white lords are pushed out of the country. He appeals to them not to get rid of caste considerations as such, but only to keep it aside for the time being: "The congress men have to swear again to speak truth [..] and put aside the idea of the holy Brahmin and the untouchable Pariah" (170). This opportunistic discourse ensured the material participation and concentration of the resources of the Bahujans in the movement and constructed a conjectural consensus of pseudo-equality and a sense of community among the nationalists and participants of the anti-colonial struggle, as has been narrated in the text.

This double speak discourse of nationalism draws liberally on the symbology of Hindu images and icons in order to perpetuate itself and to extend its boundaries of hegemony across the various regional areas of the country for laying the foundations of a Brahmanic Hindu Rashtra, through its poetry, painting, performance and even Bhajans themselves. From the *Gita* to the conch, from the spinning wheel to the Rama Rajya, the defense of Varna Dharma by Gandhi himself - every thing is predestined to be Brahmanic and hegemonic. See how these hegemonic icons are perpetuated and legitimized among the people and used to lure the Bahujans into the fold: "..blew the conch and the people came - men, women, children and the Pariah and the weavers and the potters and all seemed to feel they were of one caste, one breath" (179). The victims themselves become the Kar Sevaks of internal imperialism to fight an external enemy.

The narrative voice itself is suggestive of the divided world and worldviews. The world of the Brahmanic upper castes and that of the Dalit Bahujan never merge in the narrative discourse. The narrative voice is split between the "we" and the "Pariah." In situations of crisis the Pariah are also incorporated in to the "we" domain conjecturally and conditionally but the moment the task is achieved they are out in the margins of the narrative and the narrated reality. This again brings us to the ambiguity in the position of the Brahmanic nationalist elite and his complicit hegemonic imagination vis-a-vis the nation. His fascist, genocidal hate of the other and his liberal uplifting agency and nationalist subject position are seen to legitimize his centrality in relation to the marginality of the historic victims. As a consequence of this status quoist concern the narrative concludes only after ensuring the restoration and legitimization of hegemony and the establishment of Top Twice Born dynasties in the independent Hindi-Hindu-Hindustani-Delhi heartland. The narrative fails miserably in its set goals of making the freedom struggle a rural reality. Instead it exposes the ambiguities and double speak that the nationalist upper caste subjects practice for the reestablishment of hegemony. The narration of the Brahmanic legacy of the nationalist movement thus becomes a self-defeating task as its pedagogic objectives unveil its hegemonic history.

What is explicit here is the association between Brahmanism, caste imperialism and nationalist aspirations. For thousands of years, at least from the time of the Buddha religious conversion has been the single material solution to escape the wrath of internal caste-Varna empire and its divide-and-rule strategy. Later other alternative religions like Christianity, Islam and Sikhism lured the Bahujans with redeeming hope and egalitarian dignity. But the cursed history of the people in the peninsula remained the same as the invisible Brahmanic ideology of purity and pollution and its cultural elitism crept in through the backdoor to all the alternative religious paradigms in its unique form of disguise called caste. Even minority religions have become casteist and we have in present-day India problems concerning the Dalit Christians and Dalit Muslims.

In "Visions, Illusions and Dilemmas of Dalit Christians in India" Lancy Lobo deals with the Christian Dalit dilemma in India.[13] According to Lobo, of the 20 million Christians in India about 70 %, that is 14 million are Dalits (243). The converts suffer from four distinct types of discrimination: from the Church, from the state, from the upper castes and from the lower castes (246). So even conversion, the last resort of the downtrodden, has betrayed the historically wronged masses of India, for as Lobo says, caste is older than the church:

> There exists in each religion a wide gap between belief and practices. Christianity has no caste but Christians have caste. Therefore it is necessary that reservations are de-linked from the Hindu religion. The constitution guarantees freedom of religion and a Dalit should be free to practice any religion he or she wants. As of now if a Christian Dalit reverts to Hinduism he becomes eligible for reservations. This has made some Dalit Christians in Andhra revert to Hinduism. The bias of the state in favour of Hinduism is clear in a state that boasts of secularism [..]. Dalit Christians have developed a kind of dual identity. They have their caste identity, like Mahars and Vankars, and at the same time hyphenated labels such as Christy Mahars and Christy Vankars [..]. In general in the context of patriarchy and caste, it is admitted that just as the upper castes look down upon them, Dalit men also oppress their own women. Dalit women have to bear labour pain, produce labor power and suffer the brunt of poverty more than the men. Besides Dalit women are easy targets of rape and other atrocities from males, especially of the dominant castes. (251-6)

This is the reality of conversion in cultures in which caste system was enforced on the people to protect elite interests. Unfortunately the Christian intervention in India has produced little to improve the cultural and social status of the Bahujans, in spite of evangelist educational efforts.[14] In a way, as Lobo says, it further deteriorated the cultural crisis and the human dilemma related to identity and egalitarian dignity. This is not just a lonely voice, but the committed research that has been done in the area also agrees with this human crisis related to caste and conversion in India. In *Outside the Fold: Conversion, Modernity, and Belief* Gauri Viswanathan looks closely at this impasse of identity, and observes the importance of conversion as a form of cultural and religious critique. She also establishes the need to historicize conversion not just as a spiritual but an immensely significant political activity, the narrativization of which marks the momentous transitions to secular societies. *In Search of Identity* by Sebastian C H Kim analyzes this problematic by discussing both the missionary and the Hindutva views of conversion from the colonial era to the present. Reviewing Dick Kooiman's *Conversion and Social Equality in India: The London Missionary Society in South Travancore in the 19th Century,* M S S Pandian comments on the interaction between the Church and the colonial regime:

> While movements like Narayana Guru's rose from the ranks of the oppressed and challenged the power laden and highly differentiated local structures basing themselves fully on indigenous cultural resources (like reinterpreting Hindu religious texts) the missionary efforts were often mediations from the top and their universe of reference was never indigenous. The church and indigenous protest movements were often alternatives and not substitutes.[15]

While scholars like Tanika Sarkar argue that the colonial rule and the church compromised considerably with the Hindu Brahmanic patriarchy and the upper castes in retaining hegemony, Arunoday Guha is concerned about the double labyrinth of Christian Dalithood that robs the victims of their constitutional rights. The futility of re-conversion is the thrust of the argument in Biswamoy Pati since caste, not religion, is the key factor.[16] Lobo provides the details:

> Indigenization efforts of the church in India have been and are largely along Sanskritic lines. There are a number of reasons why the church in India has glorified Sanskritic rather than non Sanskritic tradition. Briefly (a) it had subscribed to 'down ward filtration theory', viz. you change the tip of the pyramid; (b) nationalism and patriotism were expressed in the Hindu idiom and the church was keen to throw off the colonial baggage and show itself as Indian; and (c) non Sanskritic tradition is looked down upon as mumbo jumbo, low, uncouth, rural, illiterate, backward, superstitious and inferior. Antyodaya, viz. looking at reality from the perspective of the poor, is a far cry. (256)

The question of conversion to minority religions and the problematic it initiates too have been looked at very closely by academic studies. Biswamoy Pati after looking at the history of Dalit conversion to Christianity in Orissa for the last two hundred years questions the way conversion has been located (perhaps vitally relevant in the BJP initiated debate on Conversion during 2002-03). Pati questions the basis of 're-conversion' to Hinduism since it acknowledges the reconverted as outcastes and not as caste Hindus. The question and riddle of caste in conversion is still an ongoing debate.[17] This is the socio political milieu in which we are discussing the representation of these underdogs of Indian society in a fictional narrative.

The God of Small Things is set in Kerala, where the Church boasts of a continuous history of two thousand years. The novel has already been read in several ways, as for example, as an attempt to derail hegemonic history with fictional counter history, as an attempt to distort and question the logic of the grand narrative of Kerala's historiography.[18] The first chapter itself initiates the central theme of the narrative, the caste as social evil. Estha, the boy among the two egg twins of Ammu, the central woman character in the novel, encounters the history of oppression:

> Estha walked past the village school that his grand father built for untouchable children. (13)[19]

The buried ashes of caste oppression and the history of struggles are subtly invoked and the fundamental dichotomy of touchable and untouchable human beings is introduced in to the narrative from this moment onwards. The untouchable Velutha's arrest again brings to the fore this vital question:

> It actually began thousands of years ago. Long before the Marxists came. Before the British took Malabar, before the Dutch Ascendancy, before Vasco da Gama arrived, before the Zamorin's conquest of Calicut. Before three purple-robed Syrian Bishops murdered by the Portuguese were found floating in the sea, with coiled sea serpents riding on their chests and oysters knotted in their tangled beards. It could be argued that it began long before Christianity arrived in a boat and seeped into Kerala like tea from a tea bag. That it really began in the days when the love laws were made. The laws that lay down who should be loved, and how. And how much. (33)

"Pappachi's Moth" the second chapter presents the Communist movement of Kerala and its confrontation of the caste question and how it failed totally in its class analysis in a caste-ridden society.[20] The Savarna leadership (of which Pillai and Nampoodiripadu, the mediating middle man and "high priest of communism" (67) are typical representatives from real as well as hegemonic histories), along with the touchable Syrian Christian camaraderie (among them Chacko, Ammu's communist brother is one.)

were eager to mobilize the muscle power and voting potential of the untouchables, at the same time keen to preserve the old laws of hierarchy, love laws included:

> The real secret was that communism crept into Kerala insidiously. As a reformist movement that never overtly questioned the traditional values of a caste ridden, extremely traditional community. The Marxists worked from *within* the communal divides, never challenging them, never appearing not to. They offered a cocktail revolution. A heady mix of Eastern Marxism and orthodox Hinduism, spiked with a shot of democracy. (36)

Velutha is introduced as part of a communist workers rally. He is an untouchable Paravan and a card-holding member of the party. The narrative presents the Paravans from the caste conscious Syrian Christian point of view. The Syrian Christians are ardent practitioners of untouchability, since they claim the lineage of caste Hinduism and even Brahamanism:

> As a young boy Velutha would come with Vellya Paapen to the *back* entrance of the Ayemenem house to deliver the coconuts they had plucked from the trees in the compound. Pappachi would not allow Paravans in to the house. Nobody would. They were not allowed to touch anything that touchables touched. Caste Hindus and Caste Christians. Mammachi told Estha and Rahel that she could remember a time, in her girlhood, when Paravans were expected to crawl backwards with a broom, sweeping away their footprints so that Brahmins or Syrian Christians would not defile themselves by accidentally stepping into a Paravan's footprint. In Mammachi's time, Paravans like other untouchables were not allowed to walk on public roads not allowed to cover their upper bodies, not allowed to carry umbrellas. They have to put their hands over their mouths when they spoke, to divert their polluted breath away from those whom they addressed. (73-74)

Thus the conversion into Caste Christianity was futile for the untouchables, as it is still is for the Dalits in Kerala. The narrative radically represents the undeniable dilemma of purity and pollution, and the contempt for working culture and communities shared by those self-fashioned aristocrats who survive on the labor and production of these masses. Though western intervention and colonial administration resulted in some degree of change it still survives:

> When the British came to Malabar, a number of Paravans, Pelayas and Pulayas(among them Velutha's grandfather Kelan) converted to Christianity and joined the Anglican church to escape the scourge of untouchability. As added incentive they were given a little food and money. They were known as the Rice-Christians. It didn't take them long to realize that they had jumped from the frying pan in to the fire. They were made to have separate churches, with separate services and separate priests. As a special favour they were even given their own separate pariah Bishop. After independence they found they were not entitled to any Government benefits like job reservations or bank loans at low interest rates, because officially on paper, they were Christians, and therefore casteless. It was a little like having to sweep away your footprints without a broom. Or worse, not being *allowed* to leave footprints at all. (74)

The working people were eternally subjugated and victimized and their hard labour exploited for their torture by this brutal system of social engineering. This system provided unparalleled instances of knowledge/power discourses and sites of subalternity. Nothing but life long slavery and sub human fidelity is expected and *allowed* in this system. See Vellya Paapen's existence in subalternity. He lives through it as a penance and finally informs his lords about his son's violation of the old rules and waits before his hut to kill his own young son, a loyal slave, informer and torturer of his own progeny, all in one. This is precisely what the caste system demands from the outcastes:

> Vellya Paapen however was an old world Paravan. He had seen the crawling backwards days [..] his gratitude widened his smile and bent his back. (78)

The word "touchable" is repeatedly used in the narrative to invokes its opposite, the untouchable. The repeated use of the word to refer to persons and things also inverts the whole project of purity and pollution and invokes irony. The narrative also identifies the purity-pollution core of the caste psyche in Baby Kochamma's contemptuous remark; "how could she stand the smell, these Paravans have a peculiar smell" (78).

As caste Christianity became another version of caste Hinduism, caste communism was the next to follow. Pillai and Nampoodiripadu are typical representations of caste camaraderie in Kerala. The touchable upper castes or the Savarnas and the Syrian Christians have hijacked the leadership and the decision making power in the party, that has become another Brahmanic Varnasrama or yet another church thriving on the dreams of revolution and an egalitarian society by exploiting the aspirations and man power resources of the untouchable people, the subaltern classes. Like Velutha, they owned only party cards but not power. At critical moments they were turned away unprotected from the leaders' houses like that of Pillai's. The Savarna comrades mediate between the masses, the caste, capitalism, and even the state. See the equivocations of K N M Pillai with the party workers, his business clients and the police. He is a trade union leader and a printing press owner at the same time. He prints the labels of a factory by night in which he organizes strikes of the workers by day. Regarding the arrest of his own party-man, the untouchable Velutha, he is with the touchable inspector and the system.

This feudalist, patriarchal and casteist camaraderie is under attack in the narrative. Pillai is pictured as a male chauvinist pig. His patriarchal affirmations are explicit in his dealings with his wife Kalyani, and in the way he uses her as a loyal servant and his naughty sexist puns about her made in public. When Velutha came to him at night for help he was enjoying curd and sugar with some banana. Without the trace of camaraderie he turned him away at that critical juncture and returned to another banana served specially by Kalayani. The opportunist Savarna feudal comrades' courtship with communism is further ridiculed in another inversion that tells the tale of Nampoodiripadu's old granary now turned in to a hotel (126).

This typical representation that exposes the casteist core of communism and the Brahmanical conspiracy that has permeated the epistemology in India, reminds us of Kancha Ilaiah's observation regarding the conflict between Brahmanical and Dalit Bahujan epistemologies that forms the major chunk of historic processes in India:

> In epistemological terms, the Indian nationalist discourse (pre and post independence) expressed itself in the thought process of three schools: (a) Religious nationalism of which Hinduism is the central and hegemonic school, (b) Dalit bahujan nationalism which believed in restructuring the Indian society in to a casteless, classless egalitarian sangha and (c) Communist, secular, socialist nationalism which believed in 'abolition of class' (on the European model) with a caste blind scheme of 'revolution' or transformation of the Indian society into a 'secular, socialist and communist' society. Though the first and third schools appear to be antagonistic in their discourses of transformation, the social forces that were engaged in this discourse did not differ in their roots of existence and formation. In caste/ class term they belonged to the Brahmanical upper and middle class. Though their consciousness appeared to be antagonistic to each other, their being and self remained Hindu. This was one of the main reasons why the

> Marxist and socialist schools failed to problematise and critique Hinduism and Brahmanism [..]. The post colonial Indian thus inherited two epistemological discourses, the Dalit Bahujan nationalist discourses and the Hindu nationalist discourse. Though a third school called the Marxist school emerged it remained in the hands of Brahmanical upper castes and as far as the Dalit bahujans were concerned, it remained 'a green snake in green grass'(after Kanshi Ram's expressions of the CPI(M) as the green snake in green grass and BJP as the white snake in green grass since their agenda is too explicit). (121,126)

Not just Savarna but Syrian capitalist camaraderie too is under criticism. The reference is to Chacko's "Marxist mind and feudal libido."(168). The women of the family see nothing wrong in "men's needs." They have therefore provided enough exits and doors to the house for the smooth functioning of this patriarchal practice, and even bribed the women victims:

> The enigmatic, secretly thrilling notion of men's needs gained implicit sanction in the Aymenem house. Neither Mammachi nor Babay kochamma saw any contradiction between Chacko's Marxist mind and feudal libido. They only worried about the Naxalites who had been known to force men from good families to marry servant girls whom they had made pregnant. Of course they did not even remotely suspect that the missile when it was fired, the one that would annihilate the family's good name for ever, would come from a completely unexpected quarter. (168)

See the sheer power of the patriarchal worldview in operation within the caste psyche. It is again the woman who is chained in the love laws. The man has his instinctual, legitimate needs! The question of the honour of a caste/ community is again limited and ascribed to the female sexuality and to the female body. When Chacko rapes untouchable women it is natural and when an untouchable man makes love with a touchable Christian woman it is taboo, and deadly dangerous.

How cherished and priced is this touchable identity is again illustrated in the incident of Kochumaria the cook stitching her ear lobes to preserve her Syrian Christian looks. To remain a touchable caste-Christian can be quite strenuous:

> Her right lobe had once split open and was sewn together again by Dr Verghese Verghese. Kochu Maria couldn't stop wearing her kunukku because if she did, how would people know that despite her lowly cook's job (seventy five rupees a month)she was a Syrian Christian, Mar Thomite? Not a Pulaya or a Paravan. But a touchable upper caste Christian(in to whom Christianity had seeped like tea from a teabag). Split lobes stitched back were a better option by far. (170)

While the caste conscious Christians thus stitched and re-stitched their touchable identity, the outcastes, the untouchables were pushed to the periphery for a subhuman marginal existence. The description of the subaltern hut of the Paravans is remarkable. Sensitive readers may acknowledge it as a re-writing of Asan's portrayal of Chathan's hut in *Duravastha* of the early twentieth century:

> Kuttappan, Velutha's older brother was paralysed from his chest downwards. Day after day, month after month while his brother was away and his father went to work, Kuttappan lay flat on his back and watched his youth saunter past without stopping to say hello. All day he lay there listening to the silence of huddled trees with only a domineering black hen for company. He missed his mother, Chella, who had died in the same corner of the room that he lay in now. She had died a coughing, spitting, aching phlegmy death. Kuttappen remembered noticing how her feet died long before she had. How the skin on them grew grey and lifeless. How fearfully he

> kept vigil on his own numb feet with mounting terror. Occasionally he poked at them hopefully with a stick that he kept propped up in the corner to defend himself against visiting snakes. He had no sensation in his feet at al, and only visual evidence assured him that they were still connected to his body, and were indeed his own. After Chella died, he was moved into her corner, the corner that Kuttappan imagined was the corner of his home that death had reserved to administer her deathly affairs. One corner for cooking, one for clothes, one for bedding rolls, one for dying in. (206)

But unlike his brother who was literate and able, Kuttappan "was a good, safe Paravan. He could neither read nor write" (207). That is the important thing about the untouchables, that is, as long as they remain simple, naïve and illiterate they are good. The moment they become questioning and aware of their rights, they become bad. The knowledge/power base of the hegemonic systems and discourses are subtly evoked in this remark.

So when the taboo is broken for the worse it takes the outcaste Paapen by surprise that Kochamma had touched him, as Mammachi kicks him out of her kitchen door as he informs her about the illicit relation between Velutha and Ammu, the untouchable man and touchable woman:

> He was taken completely by surprise. Part of the taboo of being an untouchable was expecting not to be touched. At least not in these circumstances. Of being locked into a physically impregnable cocoon. (256)

The touchable caste Christian spits on him and calls him dog and his caste name. The animal in him is addressed and he pledges to tear Velutha limb from limb. The touchable lady could not even imagine that:

> She imagined it in vivid detail; a Paravan's coarse black hand on her daughter's breast. His mouth on hers. His black hips jerking between her parted legs. The sound of their breathing. His particular *Paravan smell. Like*

> *animals*, Mammachi thought and nearly vomited. *Like a dog* with a bitch on heat. Her tolerance of men's needs as far as her son was concerned became the fuel for her unmanageable fury at her daughter. She had defiled generations of breeding and brought the family to its knees. (257-58)

See the beast imagery that is used to describe the outcaste in the caste imagination. It is indicative of the animal existence that is imagined and allowed in the caste worldview to the outcastes. They are not human beings belonging to the fourfold castes in Brahmanic Hinduism, but are mere animals unworthy of human rights. Another vital and key issue in caste ideology, that of endogamy too is explicitly mentioned in the passage. The notion of pure and noble breeding is central to the hegemonic claims of all elitist and fascist ideologies. Here too the touchable Caste Syrian Christian legacy has been violated and corrupted by the aboriginal sperm. But again the patriarchal double standards of this Savarna/Syrian morality is exposed in its excusing of men's needs and despising the needs of women. We are presented here with a further problematic of caste, that it is not related entirely to purity/pollution and endogamy, but is deepened by gender questions as well as by the economics of class and capital. We have seen this gender, economic and cultural capital appropriation and monopoly in the character of Pillai, who is a typical capitalist, patriarch and caste/feudal lord at the same time. This communist is with the right wing and the police in connection with the "paravan's issue" (262). He speaks the same language of the inspector, he has no doubts about the brutal treatment that should be meted out to an outcaste who violates the old hierarchy (278). His brand of comrades are working day and night to protect the hegemony and hierarchy and not to abolish them. The text prompts the suggestion that even Christianity has not deceived Keralites as Marxism did, or at least as its Savarna leadership did.

So when the touchable policemen hunts down and tortures the untouchable man it carries all these significations. The outcaste who violates the taboos has no friends. Not just men and women, even caste children abandon the outcaste. "The mother loved by night the man her children loved by day." "All three of them loved him to death." But no one loved him to save his life. That is the real tragedy of the man and his community, whom the caste system pushes out to the peripheries of existence. They are imagined, narrativized, used and eliminated. It is so easy a game, even in the present:

> Their work abandoned by god and history, by Marx, by man, by woman and by children, lay folded on the floor. He was semi conscious, but wasn't moving. His skull was fractured in three places... (310)

One striking difference in the representations regarding the gender question and the caste question in the novel is its inability to attack the social structures and worldviews presented by caste. While the narrative effectively subverts the superiority image of patriarchy and its phallocentric ideology through the technique of subversive comparisons and analogies, as in the repeated references to the "balls" of men and parallel references to the odd balls of dying dogs in the initial chapters of the novel. The male libidinal zones and centres are often reduced to banality in the narrative by adopting a kind of de-mythicization. As against the frequent references to women's body appearing in commonplace writing, repeated, seemingly casual but politically precise and targeted, references to men's body in such a way as to bring home its ugliness and beastliness is widely deployed. But unfortunately such a subversive rhetoric is nowhere in evidence in confronting the ancient hierarchies. The narrative seems already resigned to the predisposition that all this revolt is going to be wasted as the untouchable's destiny has already been stated in the first chapter. The rest is only a long excavation in to the details of the "mishap," and the spirit of confrontation and subversion shown in the representation of patriarchy is not extended to the representation of caste.

The narrative's impatience with the patriarchal worldview in other words, has not been extended to the casteist worldview. The fundamental question of caste is therefore left unanswered. Sufficient efforts are not employed to subvert its logic even from the narrative space of fiction. It is all the more important as there are many references to fiction as a flight from reality, as the point in the narrative where the twins make themselves believe that the man brutally tortured by the police before them was not Velutha but his twin brother. Taking asylum in fiction is a leit-motif in the narrative, expressed throughout as in the disguised drama of Mrs Pillai and Mrs Rajagopalan by the children earlier. Even the narrative voice seems to escape from the haunting realities of history in to the world of fiction and fantasy. That is precisely the impression the reader gets when the sexual union in all its sensuous vibrancy is presented in the last chapter, after eliminating from the scene the untouchable who violated the old taboos and love laws. He is destined to receive his "normal" punishment for his deeds (since love laws of the caste hierarchy are equated with destiny itself, at least in effect) but his forbidden fictional fantasy is being safely and submissively narrativized, without causing any challenge to the caste equilibrium.

As for the representation of the subhuman and beastly existence allowed to the outcastes, the narrative can be deemed to be splendidly successful in this endeavour. The fundamental question of social exclusion, and the exercise of power in society to engineer and control the marginality of outcastes and its maintenance: issues of control of mobility, dressing, language, education, customs, religion and worship, in addition to the practices and possibilities of inter marriage, inter dining and egalitarian social interaction, representation in political and public service and in government are contextually evoked. The representation of the untouchable hut is a typical instance of narrating marginal existence of those who are spatially and socially pushed to the periphery. The references to the untouchable school, the separate "untouchable" parish and priests for the untouchable "Christians", and the smell and the destiny of the untouchable comrade – all substantiate the most wretched and abominable of hegemonies, still eluding egalitarian resolutions. Even when fiction tries to represent the gender questions tangibly and presents a visibility to gender inequalities and violence, the question of caste, despite tremendous efforts and struggles at representing it, remains covert and invisible. It becomes elusive as in the hands of the communist camaraderie that it tries to critique. Caste becomes the un-representable in conversion. But the whole debate over conversion, its radical history and its self-defeating problematic are narrativized with its complexities as a critique of the Nation and its cultural ordering.

Notes

1. Raja Rao, *Kanthapura* (New Delhi: Orient Paperbacks, 1971), back cover.
2. Gail Omvedt, *Dalit Visions: The Anti Caste Movement and the Construction of an Indian Identity* (New Delhi: Orient Longman, 1995), specifically the chapter "Hinduism as Delhi Rule." Also see Partha Chatterjee, *The Nation and its Fragments: Colonial and Post Colonial Histories* (New Delhi: Oxford UP, 1994), the chapters "Whose Imagined Community," "The Nationalist Elite," "Communities and the Nation," "The National state" and "The Nation and Its Outcastes."
3. see Partha Chatterjee in Note 138 above. Chapters "The Nation and its Peasants", "The Nation and its Women", "Histories and the Nation", "Nation and its Pasts", "The Colonial State."
4. see Rosalind O'Hanlon, *Caste, Conflict and Ideology: Mahatma Jotiba Phule and Low caste Social Protest in Nineteenth Century Western India* (Cambridge: Cambridge

UP, 1988); Gail Omvedt, *Dalit and the Democratic Revolution: Dr. Ambedkar and the Dalit Movement in Colonial India* (New Delhi: Sage, 1994); Robin Jeffrey, "The Social Origins of a Caste Association, 1875-1905: The Founding of the S N D P Yogam," *South Asia* 4 (1974): 59-78; B R Ambedkar, *What Congress and Gandhi have Done to the Untouchables* (Bombay: T&C, 1945); J Reghu, "Adhasthitha Swathanthrya Samarngalum Heterological Histariyum," *Madhyamam Weekly* Mar. 19 (2004): 55-57; M S Jayaprakash, "Sree Narayana Guru and Social Revolution in Kerala" *Meantime* Sep. 5 (2003): 8-11. Also see Sukumar Azhikode, "Sree Narayana Guru's Abiding Relevance," *The Hindu,* Aug. 29, 2004: 5.

5. Srinivasa Iyengar, *Indian Writing in English,* 2nd ed. (New Delhi: Asia Publishers, 1973) 396, says: "it [*Kanthapura*] has a central place in Gandhian literature." Developing this, Sudhakar A. Rao in, "The Political as Spiritual: An Analysis of Kanthapura," *Socio-cultural Aspects of Life in the Selected Novels of Raja Rao* (New Delhi: Atlantic, 1999) 13-31, observes: "The villagers of Kanthapura consider Gandhian movement as holy and religious an act as the building of a temple." He also brings to the forefront the comparison of Gandhi to Lord Shiva and the equating of the freedom movement with Hindu revivalist nationalism in India. According to him "Moorthy elevates the fight for swaraj to a spiritual plane" and the novel develops "a spiritual realism." He also relates this spiritualism to Brahmanism and "Indianness." Paul Sharrad, "Indianness and Cultural Tradition," *Raja Rao and Cultural Tradition* (New Delhi: Sterling, 1987) 150-63 further develops this argument of "Vedic, Vedantic and Smritic/Brahmanic foundations of Indianness and cultural tradition," while critics like Shyamala A. Narayan in *Raja Rao: The Man and His Works* (New Delhi: Sterling, 1988) 25-43, finds "the true meaning of Brahman in Moorthy." She also identifies "social realism" in the text.

6. See Ambedkar above in Note 140. Also see his "Gandhi, Ranade, Jinnah," *The Essential Writings of B R Ambedkar*, ed. Valerian Rodriguez (New Delhi: Oxford UP, 2002) 121-32. Gail Omvedt, "Gandhi and Ambedkar,"

Economic and Political Weekly 26 (1991): 1154-55 elaborates this historical paternalism of Gandhi and the national movement which he led.

7. Gopal Guru, "Understanding Ambedkar's Construction of National Movement," *Economic and Political Weekly* 33 (1998): 156-7 says: "Ambedkar's notion of nationalism results primarily from the dichotomy between the political and the social. As is well known, the nationalist leaders, and more particularly the Hindu nationalists, laid emphasis on the political, almost ignoring the social aspect of nationalism. Ambedkar's argument was that in the absence of any comprehensive critique of the caste system and Hinduism the political is bound to suggest that the local/indigenous tyrants are preferable on 'patriotic grounds.' Emphasizing that Ambedkar was pointedly critical of nationalist Hindu homogenization, he continues: "Phule and Ambedkar were forced to adopt alternative narrative resources and dalit bahujan vocabularies which were attuned to collective struggle for both the deconstruction of the official nationalist discourse within the indigenous but egalitarian and emancipatory traditions."
8. Uma Chakravarti, "Conceptualizing Brahmanical Patriarchy in Early India," *Economic and Political Weekly* 28 (1993): 579-85.
9. M K Gandhi, *Varnasramadharma* (Bombay: Navjivan, 1962).
10. Tejaswini Niranjana, "Nationalism Refigured: Contemporary South Indian Cinema and the Subject of Feminism," *Subaltern Studies XI*, ed., Pradeep Jegannathan (New Delhi: Permanent Black, 2000) 138-66.
11. Gopal Guru, "How Egalitarian are Social Sciences in India Today?" *Economic and Political Weekly* 37 (2002): 5003-09.
12. Amartya Sen, "Basic Education: India's Backwardness and the Lessons of Kerala," *New Trends* (Kottayam: D C B, 2002) 3-8.
13. Rakesh Sharma, *Final Solution*, 2004; a documentary film on Gujarat Genocide (2002), that traces the bloody saffron trajectory of sexual violence on minority women

and even children. For a fictional rendering of the same see Rahul Dholakia's feature film *Parzania*, 2005.

14. Lancy Lobo, "Visions, Illusions and Dilemmas of Dalit Christians in India," *Dalit Identity and Politics*, Ghanashyam Shah, ed. (New Delhi: Sage, 2001) 242-49.
15. Mahatma Phule received primary education in a Missionary School in nineteenth century Maharashtra, and has acknowledged this through his life and efforts. In late nineteenth and early twentieth century Kerala, Narayana Guru has observed that the British are the ones who gave the untouchable Bahujans the right of learning and asceticism ("Sanyasam"). See K Ayyappan, *Padya Krithikal*, ed., M K Sanu. (Kottayam, D C B, 1986 (1934)), and also K A Subramanyam. And also Rosalind O'Hanlon, *Caste, Conflict and Ideology: Mahatma Jotiba Phule and Low caste Social Protest in Nineteenth century western India* (Cambridge: Cambridge UP, 1988).
16. M S S Pandian, "Church and Social Change in South Travancore," *Economic and Political Weekly* 25 (1990): 1767-68.
17. Tanika Sarkar, "Rhetoric against Age of Consent: Resisting Colonial Reason and Death of a Child wife," *Economic and Political Weekly* 28 (1993):2265-69; Arunoday Guha, "Will Mariamma's Grandson Catchup with Maramma's Grandson?," *Economic and Political Weekly* 30 (1995): 3201-02. And Biswamoy Pati in Note 18 below.
18. Biswamoy Pati, "Identity, Hegemony, Resistance: Conversions in Orissa, 1800-2000," *Economic and Political weekly* 36 (2001): 4204 -12.
19. Prasenjit Maiti, "History and Counter History: Novels and Politics," *Economic and Political Weekly* 35 (2000): 2382-85. See Sundar Sarukkai, "The Other in Anthropology and Philosophy," *Economic and Political Weekly* 32 (1997): 1406-09, for a detailed analysis that projects the validity of fiction as an ethnographic and epistemological tool , "fiction as a subjective construction of the world". See Susie Tharu and Satish Poduwal, "Refiguring Literary/Cultural Historiography," *Economic and Political Weekly* 33 (1998): 1508-09; for the erosion of disciplinary boundaries in literary and cultural studies and historiography.

20. All quotations from the text are from Arundhati Roy, *The God of Small Things* (New Delhi: India Ink, 1997).

21. See Dilip Menon, "Conjunctural Community: Communism in Malabar," *Economic and Political Weekly* 27 (1992):1934-48, for Communism's cojunctural creations of community avoiding the caste questions and its limitations and contradictions in Northern Kerala. See Gopal Guru, "Understanding Ambedkar's Construction of National Movement," *Economic and Political Weekly* 33 (1998): 156-57, for a detailed account on the cultural and social questions related to Caste rather than the economic copy book Marxist analysis of pure class categories in understanding Indian society and polity. Also see Ramakrishna Mukherjee, "Caste in itself, Caste and Class, or Caste in Class," *Economic and Political Weekly* 34 (1999):1759-61.

22. Kancha Ilaiah, "Dalitism vs. Brahmanism: The Epistemological Conflict in History," *Dalit Identity and Politics,* Ghanashyam Shah, ed. (New Delhi: Sage, 2001) 108-28.

6

Conclusion : Beyond the Margin

This dissertation began with a reference to Spivak's notion of "the marginalia," a deconstructionist critique of the centre that is repressive. The close readings and textual analyses of the selected fictional works in the previous five chapters were exclusively employed for the illustration of this marginal problematic. It will be appropriate to conclude with another of Spivak's concepts, that of "sanctioned ignorance." While attempting a critique of the Western notions of subjectivity in "Can the Subaltern Speak?" Spivak says that even Foucault, who explicated the working of the discourses of power in European clinics and prisons from the dark ages onwards, could not identify the repressive genealogy of colonial violence existing in the early twentieth century. She calls this inability to identify gross injustice and oppression in one's immediate contexts a fallacy of thought and an expression of Western metaphysics. Sanctioned ignorance is her term to denote this erasure involved in the selection of premises and prioritizing inequalities and oppressions.

Such a sanctioned ignorance can easily be identified in contemporary (fashionable) post-colonial debates taking place in India today regarding specific cultural questions of marginalization arising from gender and caste. The post colonial scholarship that furiously settles the accounts of just under two centuries of the Raj, seems to be ignorant about the millennia old caste/gender hegemony of internal Brahmanic Hindu colonialism. The simple reason for this is that the academia and the humanities, as everything else in the country, are dominated by the indigenous elites, who have taken advantage of this historical inequality and have orchestrated and are still maintaining this internal caste empire and hegemony. Any epistemological effort at problematizing the discursive contexts of cultural subordination and hegemony in academics or from outside are immediately suppressed and silenced by the status-quoist groups from the top as an exercise of the sanctioned ignorance mentioned above. This becomes more explicit if we situate this hegemonic ignorance as an epistemological violence in the historic contexts of the emergence of the voice and agency of the people, the subaltern classes in the wake of British colonial intervention.

Ethical philosophers and feminist deconstructionists like Spivak call Western colonialism an enabling wound. Spivak acknowledges its modernizing and interventionist potential for the emancipation of the subaltern from Brahmanic caste patriarchy of thousands of years. Bahujan leaders like Phule, Narayana Guru and Ambedkar welcomed and critically acknowledged Western colonialism's educational, legal and administrative reformism. Thus for the people of India two hundred years of British rule was an enabling break from the millennia old hegemony which the forces of sanctioned ignorance still perpetuate aborting the democratic politics of the people implied by such developments as the Mandal recommendations. The over-enthusiasm and academic back-up given to post-colonial studies can be seen from the people's perspective as a recent trope of these neo ignorant elites who unleashed twice-born riots in the 1990s against the inclusion of Bahujans who were excluded from the corridors of power for thousands of years. By foregrounding the two hundred years of 'suffering' by the nationalist Brahmanic elite they are erasing the struggles of the people from the 'Vedic Aryan' times to the present. This ancient hegemony that still survives as Hindu colonialism is perhaps the world's oldest and still growing trajectory of cultural subordination and internal imperialism. Thus this epistemological attempt is not post-colonial in the "sanctioned ignorance" sense, since for the women and Dalit Bahujans the anti colonial struggle against this millennia old gender/caste hegemony and imperialism is not yet over. This is a counter hegemonic and counter colonial attempt against sustaining material inequality and repressive epistemological violence from the caste/gender margins of the meta-narratives of nationalism and "post-colonialism." The discussion of texts like *Rudali* and *Gramayana* establishes this fact. The analysis of *Thalamurakal* is another complex process that problematizes the debate on the colonial/postcolonial. A view from below, from the people, from those who are in the margins of narratives, the Bahujan perspective is thus developed and utilized in the study to overcome the myopia of hegemonic consenses, that of sanctioned ignorance regarding Brahmanic colonialism. That is why the methodology of reading and analysis is always subversive and deconstructive with a polemical ethic. The critique of the dialectics of modernity mentioned in the introduction should again be contextualized from this Bahujan stand point.

As elaborated above, the identification and critical explication of the internal colonialism in fictional representations is the major epistemological outcome of the study. The caste and gender oppression/marginalization is found to be established and sustained through a sense of hierarchy and desire across religious and transcendental discourses. Brahmanic patriarchy is the key conceptual category used to elaborate the arguments here. Fiction as a socially and politically significant narrative act was found to be influenced by the material and discursive contexts of caste and gender. Both the formal as well as thematic concerns of the novel in the Indian languages are found to be shaped and determined by the material realities and associated attitudes and worldviews of caste and gender hierarchy emanating from internal imperialism. All the texts used for the discussions represent the miseries and traumas of the margins. They address questions of inequality, exclusion and exploitation. They narrativize the torturous existence of the material margins, whose struggles for egalitarian dignity are articulated in some of the committed works like *Rudali*. The analysis also reveals that works like *Kanthapura* evade and silence questions of inequality and exploitation using the form of fiction. In general all the ten novels analyzed problematize and articulate the premises of marginalization in its complexity.

Indian fictional representations (as is contemporary Indian cinema) are determined, both in terms of the message and the medium by thousands of years of cultural elitism and subordination. The themes, imagery, narrative discourse, philosophical affiliation, characterization and even the form of Indian fiction are defined by cultural elitism. Popular narratives and the mainstream cinema are equally influenced by elitist and superiority discourses. In the historic contexts of hegemony even subaltern representations tend to indulge in a kind of ventriloquism. The cultural forms and genres in our society could be seen as manifestations of the secret politics of hierarchical caste/ gender desires. Even the so called radical interventions turn out to be reiterations and reproductions of hegemonic articulations. Even popular cultural forms like mimicry and pop music reproduce hegemonic and elitist messages in Indian contexts.

This inability to come out of the hegemonic systems of representation and communication and the inadequacy of counter hegemonic significations that can subvert and resist hegemony at the micro political levels mark the general cultural crisis that overshadows writing in India today. In the light of the present study this problematic of resistance is all the more explicit. Though the ten texts chosen attempt intense critique of the gender question, the more profound and specific cultural question of caste evades comprehension and critical understanding. Caste often escapes as the un-representable in narration as it is in conversion. The narratives turn blind when it comes to the question of writing and signifying the caste problematic. A general tone of resignation and helplessness, a lethal fatalism engulfs the narratives while confronting this unique discourse. The fictional texts find it difficult to deconstruct beyond a level its genealogy of phallogocentric ethnicity, hierarchized desire, sanctioned ignorance of inequality and knowledge/ power monopolies. The cultural elitist discourses in the country that have their origin in Brahmanism and the Varna ideology play hide and seek in the narrative imagiNation and its representations. Perhaps another thousands of years of multilateral epistemological enquiry and rewriting from the Bahujan point of view would be needed for a democratic deconstruction of this hegemony.

An associated insight of this mode of enquiry is about the plurality of the margins. This is a result of the various regional manifestations of caste/gender hegemony. But across regions and linguistic/cultural terrains the Avarna communities, minority converts and women are specific targets of cultural and religious elitism throughout the peninsula. The evaluation of *Song of the Loom* given in the first chapter elaborates this point. Even minority religions are corrupted with the purity-pollution ideology of the Brahmanic Varna system. That is why we encounter upper caste elitism and gender hierarchy in Islam and Christianity in India. As the last chapter demonstrates, the Syrian Christians of Kerala boast of their Brahmanic origins even two millennia after their conversion.

Another hypothetical consideration confirmed by the study is the inseparability of gender and caste in cultural study and critique in the historic contexts of Brahmanic patriarchy. The discussion of *Rudali* proves that caste is engendered and embodied in the woman's body. The body is identified as the locus of culture and its distinctions. The body is the primal site of purity and pollution in the Indian imagiNation. It is a cultural signifier of immense semiological value in Hindu/Brahmanic colonial discursive contexts. The gaze and desire of caste/gender are focused on the body and more specifically on the phallus. The phallogocentric and ethnocentric discourses of Indian hegemony that has continued for millennia feed on the body and the governmentality of bio power. The chapter dealing with *Samskara* illustrates how internal imperialism invades the body of the sexed subaltern and eternally subordinates it as an elemental and iconic site of comprehensive control. The notorious sexual colonies of Brahmanism among Shudra women and its hegemonic functions along with the *Manudharmasastras* explain the anatomy of the psychosomatically targeted conquests.

These conquistadors who held the monopoly of religion and culture left nothing untouched. The critique of *Mavelimantam* breaks the prevalent idea that the Adivasis were left out by Brahmanism and its caste system. The fourth chapter deconstructs the tribalism and primitivism discourses that are influential in the narration of the Adivasi question. The analysis also supports the sociological notions of 'tribe into caste' and the marginalization of defiant yet broken tribes into the peripheries of culture/civilization. The hegemonic nomenclature and the divide-and-rule strategies of internal imperialism are also critically identified as the key instruments of subordination. The mediating and resolving attempts of fiction and its narrativization of historic contexts are also critically analyzed here.

Another major finding of the study is the inference regarding the resurgence of hegemony in the post-independence period. The Mandal-Mandir politics and its aftermath are invoked and contextualized in the argument. The Bahujan movements and the politics of the historically marginalized are situated in the greater contexts of constitutional democracy. Democracy is hailed here as the politics of the emerging suppressed/marginalized subjectivities. The construction of Dalit Bahujan identity and subversive subjectivity is thus radically contextualized as the grass root level democratization of the society and polity. Thus the study contests the existing formulae of hegemonic reductionism and political castration implied by terms like 'identity politics' and Sanskritization.

The study distinguishes identity and subjectivity in theoretical terms. Identity is seen as the plurality of elements that includes birth, caste/gender/class, and other regional socio cultural factors that determine an individual or group. But subjectivity is viewed as the plurality that includes the voice/language/discourse, speech/agency, mobility/potential, consciousness/unconscious, politics/ideology of the person or representative individual. In this premise subject formation is a political activity having immense implications for representation, ideology, ethics and democracy. The post-structuralist notion of decentered and plural subjectivity merges here with an element of the modernist, interventionist and consciously political subject.

The subject formation in the real sense is the politicization of the individual constitution of a being with consciousness, voice and agency, of course, in discursive contexts. And the politics of subjectivities is the democratic politics that upholds voice and agency. This democratic politics has nothing to do with mere projection and assertion of identity which is only the product of birth attributes that limit the agency and franchise of the individual. The prevalent term 'identity politics' is another perpetuation of the hegemonic groups that underrates and prevents the entry of the subaltern into political power. The term in effect erases the independent subject formation of the historically marginalized, the recognition of which is an immediate threat to hegemony. It also articulates the historical underrating of the subaltern by the dominant classes, suggesting that they could never enter into democratic politics with their collective movements that are only expressions of "identity politics."

This appropriation or hijacking effected by hegemonic nomenclature is what is sought to be exposed in the critique of Sanskritization in the context of *Thalamurakal.* According to the theory of Sanskritization that still holds currency in influential academic circles, the lower castes merely imitate the upper castes and try to go up in the hierarchical ladder. But the simple fact is that M N Srinivas's conceptual framework could not explain mobility outside the Brahmanic Hindu caste system and its meta-referential structure. It failed to explain independent community formations outside the Hindu hierarchy (that it actually erased in order to prevent the possibility of subject formations and the democratic politics of the people). And politically it aborts any possibility of the formation of solidarity among the marginalized outside the Hindu fold as in the subaltern-minority alliance or the Dalit Bahujan-women-Adivasi-minority axis. This status quoist theorization in other words is an attempt to rescue the power elite from losing historical monopolies and is itself an extension of the Hinduization project at the epistemological level. Another instance of sanctioned ignorance and epistemological violence could also be identified in this Brahmanic theorization of empirical Bahujans.

The present study also critiques the Subaltern Studies project of Partha Chatterjee and his colleagues. Even though they counter the nationalist historiography, they want to rehabilitate the struggles of the people at the heart of the nationalist anti-colonial struggles. This again is an attempt to elaborate the narrative of the nation which is dominated by the Savarna elite. The present study, in contra-distinction to this nationalist affiliation of the subaltern studies project has attempted to deconstruct this imagiNation and its discourses. It is less interested in the two hundred years of British colonialism and the Raj, and is more concerned about the thousands of years of the caste-swaraj of Brahmanic colonialism that constitute the historical discursive context of subalternity. In the study the term subaltern has additional implications. The subaltern is understood not merely as the victims of British colonialism (as testified to by Phule and Ambedkar, they were the beneficiaries of it), but of the regime of patriarchy and caste. That is why Spivak's notions of "the new subaltern" and "the gendered subaltern" are widely exploited and extended by the study to address further and profounder questions of embodied and engendered modes of subordination in Brahmanic patriarchy.

Sanskritization and other Hindu hegemonic modes of co-optive appropriations are overruled from the peoples' perspective, from the radical democratic view from below. Deconstructive, democratic and decentering modes of praxes including communitization and Dalitization along with the spirit of Mandalization are scrutinized. Communitization is only seen as the first stage of the formation of a human community that can co-exist with difference and diversity. The dissertation defines Communitization as a process of internal democratization that alleviates sub caste distinctions to form a greater egalitarian community. Further studies must be done to verify its potential to mobilize a larger human communitization process. Dalitization again is a radical levelling process involving the decolonization of the mind and culture/language from the millennia old hegemonic life practices enforced by Brahmanic colonialism. It is an egalitarian praxis that upholds self respect and ethical acknowledgement of the other. It values human dignity and the gravity of historical exclusion. It radically reverses the upward thrust of the Brahmanic caste desire and initiates an ethical vantage from below. It is downward oriented democratic decentering opposed to the concept of 'Sanskritization.' At the epistemological level it is a refashioning of the humanities and literary/cultural historiography for a subaltern hermeneutics of history and culture. All these processes are also contextualized in the broader democratization of our society, culture, human sciences, epistemology and polity.

The study itself is part of such radical democratization of epistemology and knowledge practices, especially from within the academia. This is all the more significant in a society where neo nationalist and pro fascist fundamentalism is growing and increasingly mobilizing and victimizing the people not merely through revivalist propaganda but through bloody pogroms and genocides. The sanctioned ignorance that rules the epistemological practices, as has been pointed out above, operates along with other kinds of reductionism. Economism or economic determinism is another hegemonic fashion that has suppressed the caste/ gender problematic of Indian society and culture for decades. The high priests of veiled Brahmanism and their subservient Savarna camaraderie in the Left and in the academia/media are behind this 'universalistic' class analyses. But fortunately these foot soldiers of hegemony are now in a confessional mood and are ready to recognize caste/gender as the key categories of socio cultural analysis in a traditional society devoured by Varna patriarchy.

The study has revealed, fiction as a cultural artifact evolving across the sub continent in various languages (from the early 1930s to the late 1990s) that reflects the emergency of this cultural crisis related to the marginalization of the people on caste/gender grounds. This in itself testifies to and validates the cultural implications of the study. The questions of hegemony materialized through caste/gender equations as represented in *Godan* and *Kanthapura* continue with greater force in *The God of Small Things*. Even at the close of the twentieth century O V Vijayan had to write a novel connecting the caste question with the greater ethnocentric dilemmas of the world, especially that of racism in the West. We had to wait till the twenty first century to see the first generation Dalit autobiographical narratives and fiction as in Limbale. The growing inequalities and the withdrawal of the state from constitutional liabilities in a conventional society like ours, especially in the context of neo liberalism and economic globalization intensify the miseries and struggles of the marginalized. In an increasingly unequal world which boasts of making poverty (created by Western imperialism) history, and says nothing about the race/gender inequalities and its regional manifestations like the Indian caste system that has existed from the origin of civilizations, the ethical deconstruction of epistemology and writing back from the peripheries have only just begun from the perspective of the historically marginalized. The subversive subjectivities are still in the making and the democratic cultural politics and solidarities of the people are also anticipated by this humble epistemological effort, since knowledge is power and it is subversive in the plural sense.

Selected Bibliography

Primary Works

Baby, K J. *Mavelimantam*. Thrissur: Current Books, 2000.

Bahaddur, Rao. *Gramayana*. Trans. P V Joshi. New Delhi: Sahitya Akademi, 2002.

Bismillah, Abdul. *Song of the Loom*. Trans. Rashmi Govind. Madras: Macmillan, 1996.

Devi, Mahasweta. *Rudali*. Trans. Anjum Katyal. Calcutta: Seagull, 1990.

Mukhopadhyay, Shirshendu. *Wood Worm*. Trans. Shampa Banerjee. Madras: Macmillan, 1996.

Murthy, Anantha. *Samskara: The Rite for a Dead Man*. Trans. A K Ramanujan. New Delhi: Oxford UP, 1996.

Premchand. *Godan: The Gift of a Cow*. Trans. Gordon C R. Bloomington: Indiana UP, 2002.

Rao, Raja. *Kanthapura*. New Delhi: Orient Longman, 1971.

Roy, Arundhati. *The God of Small Things*. New Delhi: India Ink, 1997.

Vijayan, O V. *Thalamurakal*. Kottayam: D C Books, 1998.

SECONDARY WORKS

Ahmad, Aijaz. *In Theory: Classes Nations Literatures*. New Delhi: Oxford UP, 1992.

Ahmed, Imtiaz. *Pluralism and Equality: Values in Indian Society and Politics*. New Delhi: Sage, 2000.

Ahmed, Irfan, ed. *Caste and Social Stratification Among Muslims*. New Delhi: Lal, 1978.

—. "A Different Jihad: Dalit Muslims' Challenge to Ashraf Hegemony." *Economic and Political Weekly* 38 (2003): 4886-91.

Ajitha, K. *Ormakkurippukal*. Kottayam: N B S, 1994.

Alam, Anwar. "Democratisation of Indian Muslims." *Economic and Political Weekly* 38 (2003): 4881-85.

Althusser, Louis. *Lenin and Philosophy and Other Essays.* Trans. Ben Brewster. London: New Left Books, 1970.

Ambedkar, B R. "Annihilation of Caste." *The Essential Writings of B R Ambedkar.* Ed. Valerian Rodriguez. New Delhi: Oxford UP, 2002. 263-78.

—. *The Buddha and his Dhamma.* Bombay: S C P, 1957.

—. *Castes in India: Speeches and Writing of Dr Babasaheb Ambedkar.* Vol. 1. Bombay: Govt. of Maharashtra, 1982.

—. *Complete Works.* Vol. 2. Bombay: Govt. of Maharashtra, 1986.

—. "Gandhi, Ranade, Jinnah." *The Essential Writings of B R Ambedkar.* Ed. Valerian Rodrigues. New Delhi: Oxford UP, 2002. 121-32.

—. *What Congress and Gandhi Have Done to the Untouchables.* Bombay: T&C, 1945.

Anand, S. "Sanskrit, English and Dalits." *Economic and Political Weekly* 34 (1999): 2053-56.

—. "Thyagaraja's Cow." *Outlook* 43. 35 (2003): 58-59.

Anderson, Benedict. *Imagined Communities: Reflections on the Origin and Spread of Nationalism.* London: Verso, 1983.

Anderson, Perry. *In the Tracks of Historical Materialism.* London: Verso, 1984.

Anderson, Walter K and Shridhar D D. *The Brotherhood in Saffron: The Rashtriya Swayamsevak Sangh and Hindu Revivalism.* New Delhi: Vistar, 1987.

Appadurai, Arjun. "Is Homohierarchicus?." *American Ethnologist* 13. 4 (1986): 745-61.

—. *Modernity at Large: Cultural Dimensions of Globalization.* Minneapolis and London: U of Minnesota P, 1996.

Arslan, Mehdi and Janki Rajan, eds. *Communalism in India: Challenge and Response.* New Delhi: Manohar, 1994.

Arunima, G. "Face Value: Ravi Varma's Portraiture and the Project of Colonial Modernity." *Indian Economic and Social History Review* 40. 1 (2003): 57-80.

Ashcroft, Bill et al., eds. *The Postcolonial Studies Reader.* London: Routledge, 1995.

Ayyappan, A. *Iravas and Cultural Change.* Madras: Govt. of Madras, 1944.

—. *Social Revolution in a Kerala Village: A Study in Cultural Change*. Bombay: Asia Publishing House, 1965.

Ayyappan, K. *Padya Krithikal*. Ed. M K Sanu. Kottayam: D C Books, 1986.

Azhikode, Sukumar. "Sree Narayana Guru's Abiding Relevance." *The Hindu*. Aug. 29 (2004): 5.

Baburaj, K K. "Identity, Alienation, Expression: Dalit Writing in Kerala." Trans. Ajay Sekher. *The Word Plus*. Jan. - Mar. (2005): 34-38.

—. "Mantakanavukalile Michasidhantham." *Mathrubhumi Weekly* 82.18 (2004): 18-23.

Bakhtin, Mikhail. "Discourse in the Novel." *Literary Theory: An Anthology*. Ed. Julie Rivkin and Michael Ryan. Oxford: Blackwell, 1998. 32-44.

—. *Problems of Dostoevksy's Poetics*. Trans. Caryl Emerson. Manchester: Manchester UP, 1984.

Balakrishnan, P K. *Jativyavastitiyum Kerala Charithravum*. Kottayam: N B S, 1986.

Bama. *Sangati: Events*. Trans. Lakshmi Homlstrom. New Delhi: Oxford UP, 2005.

Bandopadhyay, Sekhar. *Caste, Culture and Hegemony: Social Domination in Colonial* Bengal. New Delhi: Sage, 2004.

Banerjee, Sumanta. "Pitfalls of Neo Nationalism." *Economic and Political Weekly* 33 (2005): 3629-31.

Bardhan, Kalpana, ed. *Of Women, Outcastes, Peasants and Rebels*. Berkeley: U of California P, 1990.

Baudrillard, Jean. *For a Critique of the Political Economy of the Sign*. Trans. C Levin. St Louis: Telos Press, 1981.

Bauman, Zygmunt. *Postmodern Ethics*. Oxford: Blackwell, 1993.

Bayly, Susan. *Caste, Society and Politics in India from the 18th c. to the Modern Age*. Cambridge: Cambridge UP, 1999.

Beck, Tony and Tirthankar Bose. "Dispossession, Degradation and Empowerment of Peasantry and the Poor in Bengali Fiction." *Economic and Political Weekly* 30 (1995): 441-48.

Belsey, Catherine. *Critical Practice*. London: Routledge, 1980.

Benhabib, Seyla. *Situating the Self: Gender, Community and Postmodernism in Contemporary Ethics*. Cambridge: Polity Press, 1992.

Benjamin, Walter. *Illuminations*. Ed. Hannah Arendt. London: Fontana, 1970.

Bennet, Tony. *Culture: A Reformer's Science*. London: Sage, 1998.

Beteille, Andre. *Caste, Class and Power: Changing Patterns of Stratification in a Tanjore Village*. 2nd ed. New Delhi: Oxford UP, 2002.

—. *Equality and Universality: Essays in Social and Political Theory*. New Delhi: Oxford UP, 2002.

—. "Matters of Right and of Policy." *Seminar* 549 (2005):17-22.

—. "The Reproduction of Inequality: Occupation, Caste and Family." *Social Inequality in India: Profiles of Caste, Class and Social Mobility*. Ed. K L Sharma. New Delhi: Rawat, 2001, 124-32.

Bhabha, Homi. *The Location of Culture*. London: Routledge, 1994.

—, ed. *Nation and Narration*. London: Routledge, 1990.

Bharucha, Rustom. *In the Name of the Secular: Contemporary Cultural Activism in India*. New Delhi: Oxford UP, 1998.

—. "Muslims and Others: Anecdotes, Fragments and Uncertainties of Evidence." *Economic and Political Weekly* 38 (2003): 4238-50.

Bhaskar, B R P. "Adrisyarakunna Dalitar." *Kalakaumudi Weekly* 1269 (2000): 31-34.

—. "Kavyabhavanayum Charithrasathyavum." *Kalakaumudi Weekly* 1254 (1999): 43-45.

—. "Thulyathayude Sthanam Yogyathaykku Mukalil." *Kalakaumudi Weekly* 1290 (2000): 21-23.

Bhuskute, R V. "Tribals, Dalits and Government Land." *Economic and Political Weekly* 24 (1989): 2355-61.

Bourdieu, Pierre. *Distinction: A Social Critique of the Judgement of Taste*. London: Routledge, 1984.

—. "Forms of Capital." *Education: Culture, Economy and Society*. Ed. A H Halsey et al. Oxford: Oxford UP, 1986. 46-58.

—. *The Logic of Practice*. Cambridge: Polity Press, 1990.

—. *Outline of a Theory of Practice*. Cambridge: Cambridge UP, 1977.

—. *Practical Reason: On the Theory of Action*. Cambridge: Polity, 1998.

Certeau, Michel de. *Heterologies*. Trasns. Brian Massumi. Minneapolis: U of Minnesota P, 1986.

Chakrabarty, Dipesh. *Habitations of Modernity: Essays in the Wake of Subaltern Studies*. New Delhi: Permanent Black, 2002.

—. *Provincializing Europe: Postcolonial Thought and Historical Discourse*. New Delhi: Oxford UP, 1999.

Chakravarty, Uma. "Building Consent: The Middle Classes, Violence and Hindutva." *Communalism in India: Challenge and Response*. Ed. Mehdi Arslan and Janki Rajan. New Delhi: Manohar, 1994. 98-112.

—. "Conceptualising Brahmanic Patriarchy in Early India: Caste, Gender, Class and State." *Economic and Political Weekly* 28 (1993): 579-85.

—. "Saffronising the Past: Of Myths, Histories and Right Wing Agendas." *Economic and Political Weekly* 33 (1998): 225-32.

—. "Reconceptualising Gender: Phule, Brahmanism and Brahmanical Patriarchy." *Gender and Caste*. Ed. Anupama Rao. New Delhi: Sage, 2004. 164-79.

Chandra, Bipan. "Reservations and Development." *Mandal Commission Controversy*. Ed. Asgar Ali Engineer. Delhi: Ajanta, 1991. 164-70.

Chandramohan, P. "Social and Political Protest in Travancore: A Study of the SNDP (1900-1938)." M Phil Dissertation. Jawaharlal Nehru U. New Delhi, 1981.

Chatterjee, Partha. "Caste and Subaltern Consciousness." *Subaltern Studies 6*. Ed. Ranajit Guha. New Delhi: Oxford UP, 1989. 169-209.

—. *The Nation and Its Fragments: Colonial and Post colonial Histories*. Delhi: Oxford UP, 1994.

—. *Nationalist Thought and the Colonial World: A Derivative Discourse?* Delhi: Oxford UP, 1986.

Chomsky, Noam and Edward Hermann. *Manufacturing Consent: The Political Economy of the Mass Media*. London: Vintage, 1994.

Chowdhary, Prem. "Enforcing Cultural Codes: Gender and Violence in Northern India." *Economic and Political Weekly* 32 (1997): 1019-28.

Critchley, Simon. *The Ethics of Deconstruction: Derrida and Levinas*. 2nd ed. Edinburgh: Edinburgh UP, 1999.

Dalit Panthers. "Dalit Panthers' Manifesto." *Untouchable Voices of the Dalit Liberation Movement.* Ed. Barbara R. Joshi. London: Zed Books, 1986. 112-34

Damodaran, K. *Kerala Charitram: Pracheena Keralam.* Thiruvananthapuram: Prabhat, 1991.

Dangle, Arjun, ed. *Homeless in My Land.* Hyderabad: Orient Longman, 1999.

—, ed. *Poisoned Bread.* Hyderabad: Orient Longman, 1996.

Das, Veena, ed. *Communities, Riots and Survivors in South Asia.* New Delhi: Oxford UP, 1990.

Deleuze, Gilles, and Felix Guattari. *Anti Oedipus: Capitalism and Schizophrenia.* London: Athlone, 1983.

—. *A Thousand Plateaus.* Trans. Brian Massumi. London: Athlone, 1987.

Derrida, Jacques. *Dissemination.* Trans. Barbara Johnson. Chicago: Chicago UP, 1981.

—. *Of Grammatology.* Trans. Gayatri Spivak. Baltimore: Johns Hopkins UP, 1976.

—. *The Truth in Painting.* Trans. Geoff Bennington and Ian MacLeod. London: U of Chicago P, 1987.

—. *Writing and Difference.* Trans. Alan Bass. London: Routledge, 1997.

Deshpande, G P. "Metaphysics and Protest in Discourse on Buddhism." *Economic and Political Weekly* 39 (2004): 3109-10.

Deshpande, Satish. "Communalising the Nation-space: Notes on Spatial Strategies of Hindutva." *Economic and Political Weekly* 30 (1995): 3220-27.

—. "Hegemonic Spatial Strategies: The Nation Space and Hindu Communalism in Twentieth Century India." *Subaltern Studies 11: Community, Gender and Violence.* Ed. Partha Chatterjee and Pradeep Jeganathan. NewDelhi: Permanent Black, 2000. 146-62.

Deshpande, Shashi. *Writing from the Margin*. New Delhi: Penguin and Viking, 2003.

Devi, Mahasweta. *Breast Stories*. Trans. Gayatri Spivak. Calcutta: Seagull, 1992.

—. *Imaginary Maps*. Trans. Gayatri Spivak. Calcutta: Thema, 1993.

Dirks, Nicholas. *Castes of Mind: Colonialism and the Making of Modern India*. New Delhi: Permanent Black, 2002.

Dube, Leela. "Caste and Women." *Gender and Caste*. Ed. Anupama Rao. New Delhi: Sage, 2004. 223-48.

DuBois, W E B. *The Souls of Black Folk*. Chicago: A C M & Co., 1903.

Dumont, Louis. *Homo Hierarchicus: The Caste System and Its Implications*. London: Paladin, 1970.

Eagleton, Terry. *The Ideology of the Aesthetic*. Oxford: Blackwell, 1990.

—. *Ideology: An Introduction*. London: Verso, 1991.

—. *Literary Theory: An Introduction*. Minneapolis: Minnesota UP, 1983.

Eagleton, Terry, Fredric Jameson and Edward Said, eds. *Nationalism, Colonialism, Literature: A Field Day Company Book*. Minneapolis: Minnesota UP, 1990.

Easthope, Antony. *Literary into Cultural Studies*. London: Routledge, 1990.

Engineer, Asgar Ali, ed. *Mandal Commission Controversy*. Delhi: Ajanta, 1991.

—. "Remaking Indian Muslim Identity." *Economic and Political Weekly* 26 (1991): 1036-38.

Foucault, Michel. *The Archeology of Knowledge and the Discourse on Language*. Trans. A M Sheridan Smith. New York: Harper and Row, 1972.

—. *The Foucault Reader*. Ed. Paul Rabinow. London: Peregrine, 1986.

—. *The Order of Things: An Archaeology of the Human Sciences*. New York: Vintage, 1994

—. *Society Must be Defended: Lectures at the College de France 1975-76*. Trans. David Macey. New York: Picador, 2003.

Franco, F. "Ideology as Social Practice: The Fuction of Varna." *Economic and Political Weekly* 24 (1989): 2601-12.

Franco, Fernando et al., eds. *Journeys to Freedom: Dalit Narratives*. Kolkota: Samya, 2004.

Franco, Fernando, Jyotsna Macwan, and Suguna Ramanathan, eds. *The Silken Swing: The Cultural Universe of Dalit Women*. Calcutta: Stree, 2000.

Fuller, C J. *Caste Today*. New Delhi: Oxford UP, 2000.

Gandhi, M K. *Varnasramadharma*. Bombay: Navjivan, 1962.

Ganesh, K N. *Keralthinte Innalekal*. Thiruvanantapuram: Dept. of Culture, Govt of Kerala, 1990.

Geetha, V and S V Rajadurai. "Neo Brahmanism: An Intentional Fallacy?" *Economic and Political Weekly* 28 (1993): 129-36.

Gibson, Andrew. *Postmodernity, Ethics and the Novel: From Leavis to Levinas*. London: Routledge, 1999.

Gilroy, Paul. *After Empire: Melancholia or Convivial Culture*. London: Routledge, 2005.

—. *The Black Atlantic: Modernity and Double Consciousness*. London: Verso, 1993.

—. *Small Acts*. London: Verso, 2002.

—. *There Ain't No Black in the Union Jack*. London: Hutchinson, 1987.

Godelier, Maurice. "What is a Sexual Act?." *Anthropological Theory* 3. 2 (2003): 179-98.

Gopan, C. *Padham Rangavatharanthail*. Ph D Dissertation. School of Letters, M G University, Kottayam: 2002.

Guha, Arunoday. "Will Mariamma's Grandson Catchup with Maramma's Grandson?." *Economic and Political Weekly* 30 (1995): 3201-02.

Guha, Ramachandra. *An Ecological History of India*. New Delhi: Oxford UP, 2002.

—. "Savaging the Civilized: Verrier Elwin and the Tribal Question in Late Colonial India." *Economic and Political Weekly* 31 (1996): 2375-89.

Guillory, John. *Cultural Capital: The Problems of Literary Canon Formation*. Chicago: U of Chicago P, 1993.

—. "Literary Critic as Intellectual: Class Analysis and the Crisis of the Humanities." *Rethinking Class: Literary Studies and Social Formations*. Ed. Dimock and Gilmore. Columbia: Columbia UP, 1994. 145-49.

Guru, Gopal. "Corporate Class and its Veil of Ignorance." *Seminar* 549 (2005): 36-45.

—. *Dalit Cultural Movement and Dialectics of Dalit Politics in Maharashtra*. Bombay: Vikas, 1998.

—. "Dalit Movement in Mainstream Sociology." *Economic and Political Weekly* 28 (1993): 570-73.

—. "Dalits in Pursuit of Modernity." *India Another Millenium?*. Ed. Romila Thapar. New Delhi: Penguin, 2001. 123-36.

—. "Dalit Women Talk Differently." *Gender and Caste*. Ed. Anupama Rao. New Delhi: Kali for Women, 2003. 80-85.

—. "Hinduization of Ambedkar in Maharashtra." *Economic and Political Weekly* 26 (1991): 339-41.

—. "How Egalitarian are the Social Sciences in India?" *Economic and Political Weekly* 37 (2002): 5003-09.

—. "The Interface between Ambedkar and the Dalit Cultural Movement in Maharashtra." *Cultural Subordination and the Dalit Challenge: Dalit Identity and Politics*. Ed. Ghanshyam Shah. New Delhi: Sage, 2001.180-94.

—. "The Language of Dalit Bahujan Political Discourse." *Cultural Subordination and the Dalit Challenge: Dalit Identity and Politics*. Ed. Ghanshyam Shah. New Delhi: Sage, 2001. 97-107.

—. "Liberating Jotiba Phule." *Economic and Political Weekly* 38 (2003): 35.

—. "Understanding Ambedkar's Construction of National Movement." *Economic and Political Weekly* 33 (1998): 156-57.

Guru, Nataraja. *Life and Teachings of Narayana Guru, Part I: Word of the Guru*. Fernhill: East-West University, 1990.

Gramsci, Antonio. *Prison Notebooks*. Ed. Hoare and Smith. New York: International Publishers, 1989.

Gupta, Dipankar. *Mistaken Modernity: India Between Worlds*. New Delhi: Harper Collins, 2000.

Hall, Stuart. *Representation: Cultural Representations and Signifying Practices*. London: Sage, 1997.

Hanlon, Rosalind O'. *Caste, Conflict and Ideology: Mahatma Jotiba Phule and Low Caste Social Protest in 19th c. Western India*. Cambridge: Cambridge UP, 1988.

Hansen, Thomas Blom. "Globalization and Nationalist Imaginations: Hindutva's Promise of Equality." *Economic and Political Weekly* 31 (1996): 603-16.

Hardiman, David. "Subaltern Studies at Crossroads." *Economic and Political Weekly* 21 (1986): 290.

Hasan, Mushirual. "Changing position of Muslims and the political Future of Secularim in India." *Region, Religion, Caste, Gender and Culture in Contemporary India.* Ed. T V Sathyamurty. NewDelhi: Oxford UP, 1996. 200-28.

—. "'Majorities' and 'Minorities' in Modern South Asian Islam: A Historian's Perspective." *Caste and Social Stratification Among Muslims*. Ed. Imtiaz Ahmed. New Delhi: Oxford UP, 1978. 141-55.

Hasan, Zoya. "More Equal But Still Not Equal: State and Inter Group Equality in Contemporary India." *Caste and Social Stratification among Muslims*. Ed. Imtiaz Ahmed. New Delhi: Oxford UP, 1978. 82-91.

Hardt, Michael and Antonio Negri. *Empire*. Cambridge: Harvard UP, 2000.

Heredia, Rudolf C. "No Entry, No Exit: Savarna Aversion Towards Dalit Conversion." *Economic and Political Weekly* 39 (2004): 4543-55.

—. "Subaltern Alternatives on Caste, Class and Ethnicity," *Contributions to Indian Sociology* 34. 1 (2000): 37-62.

—. "Tribal History: Living Word or Dead Letter?." *Economic and Political Weekly* 35 (2000):1522-25.

hooks, bell. *Ain't I a Woman: Black Women and Feminism*. Boston: South End Press, 1981.

—. *Black Looks: Race and Representation*. Boston: South End Press, 1992.

—. *Outlaw Culture: Resisting Representation*. London: Routledge, 1994.

—. *Yearning, Race, Gender and Cultural Politics*. Boston: South End Press, 1990.

—. and Cornel West. *Breaking Bread: Insurgent Black Intellectual Life.* New York: Picador, 1991.

Human Rights Watch. *Broken People: Caste Violence Against India's Untouchables*. Bangalore: B F C, 2001.

Ilaiah, Kancha. "Beef, BJP and Food Rights of People." *Economic and Political Weekly* 31 (1996): 1444-45.

—. *Buffalo Nationalism: A Critique of Spiritual Nationalism.* Kolkota: Samya, 2004.

—. "Cow and Culture." *The Hindu*. 21 Jul. 2002.

—. "Dalitism vs. Brahmanism: The Epistemological Conflict in History." *Cultural Subordination and the Dalit Challenge: Dalit Identity and Politics,* Ed. Ghanshyam Shah. New Delhi: Sage, 2001. 108-28.

—. *Why I am Not a Hindu*. Kolkota: Samya, 1996.

Irigaray, Luce. "The Power of Discourse and the Subordination of the Feminine." *Literary Theory: An Anthology*. Ed. Julie Rivkin and Michel Ryan. London: Routledge, 2000. 34-53.

Iyengar, K R Srinivasa. *Indian Writing in English*. Rev. ed. New Delhi: Sterling, 1983.

Jaffrelot, Christophe. *Dr. Ambedkar and Untouchability*. New Delhi: Permanent Black, 2005.

—. "Hindu Nationalism and Democracy." *Democracy in India*. Ed. Nirja Jayal. New Delhi: Oxford UP, 2001. 233-41.

—. *India's Silent Revolution: The Rise of the Low Castes in North Indian Politics*. New Delhi: Permanent Black, 2003.

—. "Redressing Disadvantages: Reservation and Private Sector." *Seminar* 549 (2005): 33-35.

Jaiswal, Suvira. *Caste: Origin, Function and Dimensions of Change*. Delhi: Manohar, 1998.

Jameson, Fredric. *The Political Unconscious: Narration as a Socially Symbolic Act.* London: Methuen, 1981.

—. *Postmodernism or the Cultural Logic of Late Capitalism*. London: Verso, 1991.

Janu, C K. *Mother Forest: The Unfinished Story of C K Janu, As Told to and Written by Bhaskaran*. Trans. Ravi Shankar. New Delhi: Women Unlimited and Kali for Women, 2004.

Jayal, Niraja, ed. *Democracy in India.* New Delhi: Oxford UP, 2001.

Jayaprakash, M S. "Sree Narayana Guru and Social Revolution in Kerala." *Meantime* 5.10 (2003): 8-11.

—."Sanchara Swathanthriavum Dalavakkulam Koottakkolayum." *Madhyamam Weekly* 7. 22 (2004): 4.

Jeffrey, Robin. *The Decline of Nayar Dominance: Society and Politics in Travancore; 1847-1908.* New York: Macmillan, 1976.

—. *Politics, Women and Wellbeing: How Kerala Became a 'Model.'* New Delhi: Oxford UP, 1992.

—. "The Social Origins of a Caste Association; 1875-1905: The Founding of the SNDP Yogam." *South Asia* 4 (1974): 59-78.

Jenkins, Keith. *Rethinking History.* London: Routledge, 2003.

—. *Why History: Ethics and Postmodernity.* London: Routledge, 1998.

Jenkins, Richard. *Pierre Bourdieu.* London: Routledge, 1992.

Jogdand, P G, ed. *New Economic Policy and Dalits.* New Delhi: Rawat, 2000.

Jondhle, Surendra and Johannes Beltz, eds. *Reconstructing the World: B R Ambedkar and Buddhism in India.* New Delhi: Oxford UP, 2004.

Joshi, Umashankar. *The Idea of Indian Literature.* New Delhi: Sahitya Akademi, 1990.

Kakar, Sudhir. "Some Unconscious Aspects of Ethnic Violence in India," *Communities, Riots and Survivors in South Asia.* Ed. Veena Das. New Delhi: Oxford UP, 1990. 135-44.

Kannabiran, Vasantha and Kalpana Kannabiran. "Caste and Gender: Understanding Dynamics of Power and Violence." *Economic and Political Weekly* 26 (1991): 2130-33.

—. *De-Eroticizing Assault: Essays on Modesty, Honour and Power.* Kolkota: Stree, 2002.

Kaplan, Ann. *Looking for the Other: Feminism, Film and the Imperial Gaze.* New York: Routledge, 1997.

Kapstein, Mathew T, ed. *Buddhism Omnibus.* New Delhi: Oxford UP, 2004.

Kapur, Geeta. *When Was Modernism: Essays on Contemporary Cultural Practice in India.* New Delhi: Tulika, 2001.

Katyal, Anjum. "The Metamorphosis of Rudali." *Rudali*. By Mahasweta Devi. Calcutta: Seagull, 1997. 1-53.

Kaviraj, Sudipta. "Imaginary Institution of India." *Subaltern Studies 7*. New Delhi: Oxford UP, 1992. 16-19.

Kesavadev, P. *Ethirpu*. Thiruvananthapuram: Prabhat, 1999.

Kesavan, C. *Jeevitasamaram*. Kottayam: N B S, 1990.

Kim, Sebastian C H. *In Search of Identity*. New Delhi: Oxford UP, 2003.

Kochu, K K. "A Dalit Reading of Sri Narayana Movement." Trans. Ajay Sekher. *The Word Plus*. Jan. - Mar. (2005): 39-44.

—. "Swathutamastatayute Avirbhavam." *Madhyamam Weekly* 4.32 (2002): 23-27.

Kooiman, Dick. *Conversion and Social Equality in India: The London Missionary Society in South Travancore in the 19th Century*. New Delhi: Manohar, 1989.

Kosambi, D D. "Caste and Class in India." *D D Kosambi on History and Society: Problems of Interpretation*. Ed. A J Syed. Bombay: U of Bombay, 1985. 233-54.

—. "The Possible Sources of the Gita." *Combined Methods in Indology and Other Writings: D D Kosambi*. Ed. B Chathopadhyaya. New Delhi: Oxford UP, 2002. 373-90.

Lacan, Jacques. *Ecrits: A Selection*. Trans. Alan Sheridan. London: Tavistock, 1977.

—. *The Four Fundamental Concepts of Psychoanalysis*. Trans. Alan Sheridan. London: Hogarth Press, 1979.

Laclau, Ernesto. *New Reflection on the Revolution of Our Time*. London: Verso, 1990.

Laclau, Ernesto, and Chantal Mouffe. *Hegemony and Socialist Strategy: Towards a Radical Democratic Politics*. London: Verso, 1985.

Limbale, Sharankumar. *Towards an Aesthetic of Dalit Literature: History, Controversies and Considerations*. Trans. Alok Mukherjee. New Delhi: Orient Longman, 2004.

Lobo, Lancy. "Visions, Illusions and Dilemmas of Dalit Christians in India." *Dalit Identity and Politics*. Ed. Ghanashyam Shah. New Delhi: Sage, 2001. 242-49.

Lodge, David, ed. *Modern Criticism and Theory: A Reader*. London: Longman, 1998.

—. *After Bakhtin: Essays in Fiction and Criticism*. London: Routledge, 1990.

Lukacs, Georg. *The Theory of the Novel*. Trans. Anna Bostock. London: Merlin, 1971.

Lynch, Owen. *The Politics of Untouchability*. New York: Colombia UP, 1969.

Lyotard, Jean Francois. *The Postmodern Condition: A Report on Knowledge*. Trans. Geoff Bennington and Brian Massumi. Manchester: Manchester UP, 1984.

Mahajan, Gurpreet. *Identities and Rights: Aspects of Liberal Democracy in India*. New Delhi: Oxford UP, 2001.

Maiti, Prasenjit. "History and Counter History: Novels and Politics." *Economic and Political Weekly* 35 (2000): 2382-85.

Malcom X and Alex Haley. *The Autobiography of Malcom X*. New York: Grove Press, 1965.

Manudharma Sastra or Laws of Manu. Trans. George Buhler. Delhi: Munshiram, 1984.

Mencher, J. "On Being an Untouchable in India: A Materialist Perspective." *Beyond the Myths of Cultural Materialism*. Ed. Eric Ross. New York: Academic Press, 1980. 24-33.

—. "Viewing Hierarchy from the Bottom Up." *Encounter and Experience: Personal Accounts of Fieldwork*. Ed. Andre Beteille. New Delhi: Vikas, 1975. 114-30.

Menon, Dilip. *Caste, Nationalism and Communism in South Inida*. Cambridge: Cambridge UP, 1994.

—. "Conjunctural Community: Communism in Malabar." *Economic and Political Weekly* 27 (1992):1934-48.

Misra, Amalendu. *Identity and Religion: Foundations of Anti-Islamism in India*. New Delhi: Sage, 2005.

Mondel, Seik Rahim. "Social Structure, OBCs and Muslims." *Economic and Political Weekly* 38 (2003): 4892-97.

Moon, Vasant. *Growing up Untouchable in India: A Dalit Autobiography*. Trans. Gail Omvedt. New Delhi: Vistar, 2002.

Morrison, Toni. *Playing in the Dark: Whiteness and Literary Imagination*. Cambridge: Harvard UP, 1992.

Mukherjee, Meenakshi. *Realism and Reality: the Novel and Society in India*. New Delhi, Oxford UP, 1985.

—. *The Twice-Born Fiction: Themes and Techniques of the Indian Novel in English*. New Delhi: Heinemann, 1971.

Mukherjee, Ramakrishna. "Caste in Itself, Caste and Class, or Caste in Class." *Economic and Political Weekly* 34 (1999):1759-61.

Mukherjee, Sujit. *Towards a Literary History of India*. Simla: II A S, 1975.

Munslow, Alun. *Deconstructing History*. London: Routledge, 2002.

Nabar, Vrinda. *Caste as Woman*. New Delhi: Penguin, 1995.

Nagaraj, D R. *The Flaming Feet: A Study of the Dalit Movement*. Bangalore: South Forum Press, 1993.

Nancy, Jean Luc. *Inoperative Community*. Minneapolis: U of Minnesota P, 1991.

Nanda, Meera. *Prophets Facing Backward: Postmodern Critiques of Science and Hindu Nationalism*. New Delhi: Permanent Black, 2004.

Narasimhaiah, C D. Introduction. *Kanthapura* by Raja Rao. 2nd ed. Madras: Oxford UP, 1974. xi.

Narayan, Badri and A R Misra, eds. *Multiple Marginalities: An Anthology of Dalit Writings*. Delhi: Manohar, 2004.

Narayan, Shyamala A. *Raja Rao: Man and His Works*. New Delhi: Sterling, 1988.

Natarajan, Nalini. "Gender, Caste and Modernity: A Reading of U R Ananthamurthy's Samskara in its Intellectual Context." *Sign Posts*. Ed. Rajeswari Sundar Rajan. New Delhi: Kali for Women, 1999. 154-86.

Nazir, Pervaiz. "Social Structure, Ideology and Language: Caste Among Muslims." *Economic and Political Weekly* 28 (1993): 2897-99.

Niranjana, Seemanthini. *Gender and Space: Femininity, Sexualization and the Female Body*. New Delhi: Sage, 2001.

Niranjana, Tejaswini. "Nationalism Refigured: Contemporary South Indian Cinema and the Subject of Feminism." *Subaltern Studies 11*. Ed. Pradeep Jegannathan and Partha Chatterjee. New Delhi: Permanent Black, 2000. 138-66.

Omvedt, Gail. "Ambedkar and After: The Dalit Movement in India." *Cultural Subordination and the Dalit Challenge: Dalit Identity and Politics*. Ed. Ghanshyam Shah. New Delhi: Sage, 2001. 143-59.

—. "The Anti Caste Movement and the Discourse of Power." *Democracy in India*. Ed. Nirja Jayal. New Delhi: Oxford UP, 2001. 481-508.

—. *Buddhism in India: Challenging Brahmanism and Caste*. New Delhi: Sage, 2005.

—. "Caste and Hinduism." *Economic and Political Weekly* 38 (2003): 5003-04.

—. *Dalit and Democratic Revolution: Dr Ambedkar and the Dalit Movement in Colonial India*. New Delhi: Sage, 1994.

—. *Dalit Visions: The Anti Caste Movements and the Construction of an Indian Identity*. Madras: Orient Longman, 1995.

—. "Gandhi and Ambedkar." *Economic and Political Weekly* 26 (1991): 1154-55.

—. "Hinduism and Politics." *Economic and Political Weekly* 25 (1991): 723-27.

—. "Pseudo Secularism." *The Hindu*. Jan. 20 &21, 2003.

—. "Revolutionary Music of India." *Journal of Peasant Studies* 4. 3 (1977): 243-57.

—. "Twice Born Riot Against Democracy." *Mandal Commission Controversy*. Ed. Asgar Ali Engineer. Delhi: Ajanta, 1991. 6-25.

Osella, Filippo and Caroline Osella. "Articulation of Physical and Social Bodies in Kerala." *Contributions to Indian Sociology* 30. 1 (1996): 37-68.

—. *Social Mobility in Kerala: Modernity and Idenity in Conflict*. London: Pluto, 2000.

Pai, Sudha. *Dalit Assertion and the Unfinished Democratic Revolution: The Bahujan Samaj Party in UP*. New Delhi: Sage, 2002.

Pandey, Gyanendra. "The Colonial Construction of 'Communalism': British Writings on Banaras in the Nineteenth Century." *Communities, Riots and Survivors in South Asia*. Ed. Veena Das. New Delhi: Oxford UP, 1990. 94-134.

—. *The Construction of Communalism in Colonial North India*. New Delhi: Oxford UP, 1990.

—. "Nationalism, Communalism and the Struggle over History." *Communalism in India: Challenge and Response*. Ed. Mehdi Arslan and Janki Rajan. New Delhi: Manohar, 1994.134-56.

Pandian, M S S. "Church and Social Change in South Travancore." *Economic and Political Weekly* 25 (1990): 1767-68.

Panikkar, K N. *Culture, Ideology, Hegemony*. New Delhi: Tulika, 1995.

—. "Protohistory of Hindutva." *The Hindu*. Mar. 2 (2004): 13.

Pati, Biswamoy. "Identity, Hegemony, Resistance: Conversions in Orissa, 1800-2000," *Economic and Political weekly* 36 (2001): 4204 -12.

—. "Women, Rape and the Left." *Economic and Political Weekly* 26 (1991): 219-20.

Pavithran, P. *Asan Kavitha: Adhunikananthara Padhangal*. Thiruvananthapuram: Dept. of Cultural Publications, 2002.

Phule, Jotiba. *Samagra Wanghmay*. Bombay: Govt. of Maharashtra, 1990.

Pinto, Stany. "Communalization of Tribals in South Gujrat." *Economic and Political Weekly* 30 (1995): 2416-19.

Pooncha, Veena. "Why Women Fear Religious Fundamentalism: Hindutva's Hidden Agenda." *Economic and Political Weekly* 28 (1993): 438-39.

Radhakrishnan, P. "Backward Castes/Classes as Legal and Political Entities." *Oxford India Companion to Sociology and Social Anthropology*. Ed. Veena Das. New Delhi: Oxford UP, 2003. 1474-93.

Raghavan, Puthupally. *Viplavasmaranakal III*. Kottayam: D C Books, 1995.

Rajagopal, Arvind. "The Rise of National Programming: The Case of Indian Television." *Media, Culture and Society*. Jan. (1993): 68-76.

Rajan, Rajeswari Sunder. "Is the Hindu Goddess a Feminist." *Economic and Political Weekly* 33 (1998): 34-38.

—. *Real and Imagined Women: Gender, Culture, Post colonialism*. London: Routledge, 1998.

—, ed. *Sign Posts: Gender Issues in Post Independence India*. New Delhi: Kali for Women, 1999.

Ramadas, Cherai. "Adhunika Keralthinte Srushtakkalaru?." *Mathrubhumi Weekly* 82.33 (2004): 36-40.

Rao, Anupama. "Introduction: Caste, Gender and Indian Feminism" *Gender and Caste*. New Delhi: Kali for Women, 2003. 1-17.

Rao, Sudhakar A. "The Political as Spiritual: An Analysis of Kanthapura." *Socio-cultural Aspects of Life in the Selected Novels of Raja Rao*. New Delhi: Atlantic, 1999. 13-31.

Rasmussen, David, ed. *Universalism vs. Communitarianism*. Cambridge: MIT P, 1992.

Raveendran, P P. *Aadhunikananthararam: Vicharam Vaayana*. Trichur: Current, 1999.

—. *Edapedalukal: Sahityam, Sidhantam, Rashtreeyam*. Kottayam: D C Books, 1997.

—. "Fiction and Reception: Reconstructions of the *Mahabharatha* in Malayalam." *Indian Literature* 49. 1 (2005): 152-61.

—. *Indian Literature: Readings from the Margin*. Hyderabad: Orient Longman, Forthcoming.

—. *Michel Foucault: Varthamanthinte Charithram*. Thiruvananthapuram: K L I, 2002.

—. "Politics in the Malayalam Novel: A Reading of C R Parameswaran's *Prakrutiniyamam*." *Indian Literature* 38. 5 (1995): 156-59.

—. *Samskara Padhanam: Oramukham*. Kottayam: D C Books, 2003.

Rege, Sharmila. "Dalit Women Talk Differently: A Critique of Difference and towards a Dalit Feminist Stand Point Position." *Economic and Political Weekly* 33 (1998): 39-46.

—. *Sociology of Gender*. New Delhi: Sage, 2003.

Reghu, J. "Understanding Community: Viswakarmas." *Economic and Political Weekly* 38 (2003): 5304.

—. "Adhunika Keralavum Samudaya Rupavatkaranavum." *Madhyamam Weekly* 7.7 (2004): 28-31.

—. "Adhasthitha Swathanthrya Samarngalum Heterological Histariyum." *Madhyamam Weekly* 7.12 (2004): 55-57.

—. "Hindu Colonialisavum Dalitatvavum." *Mathrubhumi Weekly* 83.28 (2005): 26-29.

—. "Hindu Colonialisavum Jativimarsavum." *Madhyamam Weekly* 6.42 (2003): 28-32.

Robinson, Rowena and Sathianandan Clarke, eds. *Religious Conversion in India: Modes, Motivations and Meanings*. NewDelhi: Oxford UP, 2003.

Report of the Joint Delegation of Women's Organizations. "Women and Communal Riots." *Communalism in India: Challenge and Response*. Ed. Mehdi Arslan and Janki Rajan. New Delhi: Manohar, 1994. 157-77.

Robb, Peter, ed. *Dalit Movements and the Meaning of Labor in India*. New Delhi: Oxford UP, 1999.

Roy, Arundhati. *The Algebra of Infinite Justice*. New Delhi: Penguin, 2001.

—. *The End of Imagination*. Kottayam: DC Books, 1998.

—. *The Greater Common Good*. Bombay: Indian Book, 1999.

—. *An Ordinary Person's Guide to Empire*. New Delhi: Penguin/ Viking, 2005.

Said, Edward. *Orientalism*. New York: Pantheon, 1978.

—. *Culture and Imperialism*. London: Verso, 1992.

Said, Edward and Raymond Williams. "Media, Margins and Modernity." *The Politics of Modernism: Against the New Conformists*. London: Verso, 1989. 177-97.

Sainath, P. "Bombay Riots of December 1992: A Report." *Communalism in India: Challenge and Response*. Ed. Mehdi Arslan and Janki Rajan. New Delhi: Manohar, 1994. 191-98.

—. "Communalism and the Media." *Communalism in India: Challenge and Response*. Ed. Mehdi Arslan and Janki Rajan. New Delhi: Manohar, 1994.136-39.

Sangari, Kumkum and Uma Chakravarty, eds. *From Myth to Markets: Essays on Gender*. New Delhi: Manohar and I I A S, 2001.

Sanu, M K. *Sahodaran K Ayyappan*. Kottayam: D C Books, 1986.

Sarkar, Sumit. *Beyond Nationalist Frames: Relocating Post Modernism, Hindutva, History*. New Delhi: Permanent Black, 2002.

—. "The BJP Bomb and Aspects of Nationalism." *Economic and Political Weekly* 33 (1998): 1725-30.

—. "The Fascism of the Sangh Parivar," *Economic and Political Weekly* 28 (1993): 163-67.

—. "Indian Nationalism and the Politics of Hindutva." *Making India Hindu*. Ed. Ludden D. New Delhi: Oxford UP, 1997. 154-68.

—. *Writing Social History*. New Delhi: Oxford UP, 1997.

Sarkar, Sumit and Pradeep Dutta. "Manufacturing Hatred: The Image of the Muslim in the Ramjanmabhumi Movement." *Communalism in India: Challenge and Response*. Ed. Mehdi Arslan and Janki Rajan. New Delhi: Manohar, 1994. 83-89.

Sarkar, Tanika. "Reflections on Birati Rape Cases: Gender Ideology in Bengal." *Economic and Political Weekly* 26 (1991): 215-18.

—. "Rhetoric Against Age of Consent: Resisting Colonial Reason and Death of a Child Wife." *Economic and Political Weekly* 28 (1993):2265-69.

Sarukkai, Sundar. "The Other in Anthropology and Philosophy." *Economic Political Weekly* 32 (1997):1406-09.

Sau, Ranjit. "Recognition to Witchcraft: Illegal and Ill-founded." *Economic and Political Weekly* 38 (2003): 5325-26.

Schroder, Ingo W. "The Political Economy of Tribalism in North America: Neotribal Capitalism?" *Anthropological Theory* 3. 4 (2003): 435-56.

Sekher, Ajay. "Monopolizing and Policing Culture: Savarna/Upper caste Hindu Hegemonic Discourse in Malayalam Media." *New Quest* 150 (2003): 43-55.

—. "Older than the Church: Caste and Christianity in the *God of Small Things*." *Economic and Political Weekly* 38 (2003): 3445-49.

Sen, Alok Parasher, ed. *Subordinate and Marginal Groups in Early India*. New Delhi: Oxford UP, 2004.

Sen, Amartya. "Basic Education: India's Backwardness and the Lessons of Kerala." *New Trends*. Kottayam: D C Books, 2002. 3-8.

Sen, Nabaneeta Dev. Introduction. *Woodworm*. By Sirshendu Mukhopadhyay. Trans. Shampa Banerjee. Madras: Macmillan India, 1996. 1-12.

Sethi, Rumina. *Myths of the Nation: National Identity and Literary Representation*. New Delhi: Oxford UP, 1999.

Shah, Ghanshyam. Ed. *Cultural Subordination and the Dalit Challenge: Dalit Identity and Politics*. New Delhi: Sage, 2001.

—. Introduction. *Caste and Democratic Politics in India*. New Delhi: Permanent Black, 2003. 5-27.

Shah, Purvi. "Scripting the Subaltern." *The Minnesota Review* 55. 57 (2002): 351-55.

Sharma, Govind Narain. *Premchand: Novelist and Thinker*. Delhi: Pragati, 1999.

Sharma, Jyotirmaya. *Hindutva: Exploring the Idea of Hindu Nationalism*. NewDelhi: Viking and Penguin, 2003.

Sharma, K L. Ed. *Social Inequality in India: Profiles of Caste, Class and Social Mobility*. New Delhi: Rawat, 2001.

Sharrad, Paul. *Raja Rao and Cultural Tradition*. New Delhi: Sterling, 1987.

Sinfield, Alan. *Cultural Politics: Queer Reading*. London: Routledge, 1994.

Singh, Rana. "Weaver's World: The Threadbare Shawl of Abdul Bismillah." *Where Cultural Symbols Meet: Images of Varanasi*. Varanasi: Tara, 1989. 24-45.

Sondhi, M L and Apratim Mukherjee, eds. *The Black Book of Gujarat*. New Delhi: Manak Publishers, 2002.

Spivak, Gayatri. "Can the Subaltern Speak." *Marxism and the Interpretation of Culture*. Ed. Carry Nelson and Lawrence Grossberg. Urbana: U of Illinois P, 1988. 51-88.

—. "Explanation and Culture: Marginalia." *In Other Worlds: Essays in Cultural Politics*. New York: Routledge, 1988. 103-17.

—. Introduction. *Breast Stories*. By Mahasweta Devi. Calcutta: Seagull, 1992. 1-12.

—. "A Literary Representation of the Subaltern: A Woman's Text from the Third world." *In Other Worlds: Essays in Cultural Politics*. NewYork: Routledge, 1988. 241-66.

—. "On the New Subaltern." *Subaltern Studies 11*. Ed. Partha Chatterjee and Pradeep Jagannathan. New Delhi: Permanent Black, 2000. 305-34.

—. *The Postcolonial Critic: Interviews, Strategies, Dialogues*. Ed. Sarah Harasym. London: Routledge, 1990.

—. "Post Structuralism and Marginality." *Contemporary Post Colonial Theory*. Ed. Padmini Mongia. London: Arnold, 1996. 132-55.

—. "Subaltern Studies: Deconstructing Historiography." *Subaltern Studies 4*. Ed. Ranajit Guha. New Delhi: Oxford UP, 1985. 338-63.

Subramanyam, K A. *Sahodaran Ayyappan*. Kochi: K A Subramanyam and Kerala Sahitya Akademi, 1976.

Sundar, Nandini. "Teaching to Hate: RSS' Pedagogical Programme." *Economic and Political Weekly* 39 (2004): 1605-12.

Srinivas, M N. *Caste in India and Other Essays*. Bombay: Asia Publishers, 1962.

—. "Gandhi's Religion." *Economic and Political Weekly* 30 (1995): 376.

—. *Village, Caste, Gender and Method: Essays in Indian Social Anthropology*. New Delhi: Oxford UP, 1996.

Thapar, Romila. *Narratives and the Making of History: Two Lectures*. New Delhi: Oxford UP, 2000.

Tharu, Susie. "The Impossible Subject: Caste and the Gendered Body." *Economic and Political Weekly* 31(1996): 1311-15.

Tharu, Susie, and K Lalitha, eds. *Women Writing in India*. 2 Vols. New Delhi: Oxford UP, 1996.

Tharu, Susie, and T Niranjana. "Problems of a Contemporary Theory of Gender," *Social Scientist* 22 (1994): 232-36.

Tharu, Susie, and Satish Poduval. "Refiguring Literary/Cultural Historiography," *Economic and Political Weekly* 33 (1998): 1508-09.

Thirumaavalavan. *Talisman: Extreme Emotions of Dalit Liberation*. Kolkota: Samaya, 2004.

Upadhyay, Shashi Bhushan. "Representing the Underdogs: Dalits in the Literature of Premchand," *Studies in History* 18. 1 (2002): 51-80.

Varghese, George. "Writing Family Histories: Identity Construction Among Syrian Christians." *Economic and Political Weekly* 39 (2004): 897-900.

Velayudhan, P S. *S N D P Yogacharitram*. Kollam: S N D P Y, 1978.

Viswanathan, Gauri. *Masks of Conquest: Literary Study and British Rule in India*. New York: Columbia UP, 1989.

—. *Outside the Fold: Conversion, Modernity and Belief*. NewDelhi: Oxford UP, 2001.

Viswanathan, S. *Dalits in Dravidian Land: Frontline Reports on Anti-Dalit Violence in Tamil Nadu 1995-2004*. Chennai: Navyana, 2005.

West, Cornel. *The Ethical Dimensions of Marxist Thought*. London: Verso, 1991.

—. *Keeping Faith: Philosophy and Race in America*. New York: Routledge, 1994.

—. *Prophetic Reflections: Notes on Race and Power in America*. New York: Routledge, 1993.

—. *Race Matters*. London: Routledge, 1993.

—, ed. *Out There: Marginalization and Contemporary Cultures*. New York: Routledge, 1990.

Williams, Raymond. *Culture and Society*. Harmondsworth: Penguin, 1957.

—. *Culture*. London: Collins, 1981.

—. *The English Novel from Dickens to Lawrence*. London: Hogarth, 1985.

—. "Forms of English Fiction in 1848." *Literature, Politics and Theory*. Eds. Francis Barker, et al. London: Methuen, 1986. 1-16.

—. *Keywords*. London: Collins, 1976.

—. *The Politics of Modernism*. London: Verso, 1989.

Xaxa, Verginius. "Tribes as Indegenous People of India." *Economic and Political Weekly* 34 (1999): 3589-95.

Zainuddin, Sayyed. "Islam, Social Stratification and Empowerment of Muslim OBCs." *Economic and Political Weekly* 38 (2003): 4898-99.

Zelliot, Eleanor. *From Untouchable to Dalit: Essays on the Ambedkar Movement*. Madras: Orient Longman, 1994.

—. "The Meaning of Ambedkar." *Cultural Subordination and the Dalit Challenge: Dalit Identity and Politics*. Ed. Ghanshyam Shah. New Delhi: Sage, 2001. 129-42.

Zizek, Slovoj. *The Sublime Object of Ideology*. London: Verso, 1989.

Index

N

O

P

R

S